Edible Wild Plants and Herbs

Trees

Shrubs

Forbs

Edible
Wild Plants and Herbs
A Ragged Mountain Press Pocket Guide

Alan M. Cvancara

Grasslike
Plants

Lichens

Seaweeds

Ragged Mountain Press / McGraw-Hill
Camden, Maine • New York • Chicago • San Francisco • Lisbon •
London • Madrid • Mexico City • Milan • New Delhi • San Juan •
Seoul • Singapore • Sydney • Toronto

Look for the next Ragged Mountain Press Pocket Guides:
Backpacking, Chris Townsend
Sea Kayaking, Shelley Johnson

Ragged Mountain Press

A Division of The McGraw-Hill Companies

10 9 8 7 6 5 4 3 2 1

Copyright © 2001 Ragged Mountain Press

All rights reserved. The publisher takes no responsibility for the use of any of the materials or methods described in this book, nor for the products thereof. The name "Ragged Mountain Press" and the Ragged Mountain Press logo are trademarks of The McGraw-Hill Companies. Printed in the United States of America.

Cvancara, Alan M.
    Edible wild plants and herbs / Alan M. Cvancara.
        p.   cm. — (A Ragged Mountain Press pocket guide)
    ISBN 0-07-136827-2 (alk. paper)
        1. Wild plants, Edible. I. Title. II. Series.
    QK98.5A1 C83 2001
    581.6′32—dc21   00-067337

Questions regarding the content of this book should be addressed to
Ragged Mountain Press
P.O. Box 220
Camden, ME 04843
www.raggedmountainpress.com

Questions regarding the ordering of this book should be addressed to
The McGraw-Hill Companies
Customer Service Department
P.O. Box 547
Blacklick, OH 43004
Retail customers: 1-800-262-4729
Bookstores: 1-800-722-4726

This book is printed on 70# Citation by R. R. Donnelley
Design by Anton Marc
Production Management by Janet Robbins
Edited by Tom McCarthy and Justine Rathbun

Band-Aid, Potable Aqua, and Velcro are registered trademarks.

Photographs by the author except where noted otherwise

As before, to Ella,
whose help and support enabled me
to complete this book

Contents

Preface

The pursuit of wild plant foods, foremost, can be fun: another way to recreate in the Great Outdoors. While we enjoy ourselves, we experience the satisfaction of nourishing ourselves in a fundamental way as did our ancestors. And, at the same time, we become closer to our natural environment and more knowledgeable about it. Further, if we realize a particular habitat harbors useful food plants, we are less inclined to deface or destroy that habitat. Aware that a marsh contains edible cattails and wild mint, we are less apt to drain it.

Equipped with the information in this book, take your young friends, children, or grandchildren on wild plant food-seeking excursions. Instill in them, by this means, a love of nature and help them become conversant with their natural environment. These can be lasting experiences from which young naturalists can develop into better guardians of their surroundings.

This book focuses on readily recognizable wild plants that can quiet your hunger with little expenditure of energy should you desire to partake in nature's supermarket. A no-nonsense approach gives you quick information in a concise style and omits unnecessary details. This book's small size and format allow you to stow it easily in your jacket, pack, or glove compartment. Trust it as a dependable companion.

CONSERVATION ETHIC

Always be conservation-conscious when you harvest wild edible plants. Even during an emergency, you can use plants with a conserving manner. Don't girdle a tree or cut away the bark in a complete circle when you are after the inner bark; otherwise the tree will die. Avoid breaking off branches in order to speed up the process while picking berries. Other prudent procedures will come to mind.

Practice restraint when exploiting wild plant foods. Gluttony here is as inexcusable as the hunter or angler who greedily takes more than the legal limit or more than either can consume. Leave some for other humans as well as for those creatures that might depend on such food. In your harvesting, always leave enough so that a plant species can reproduce and repopulate itself. And above all, don't extract wild plants for personal gain or profit; purple coneflower roots have been indiscriminately collected from prairie lands for such reasons, severely decreasing the plant's populations.

On public land, avoid collecting plants adjacent to hiking trails or motorized trails and roads. No one visiting a scenic area likes to come across plants or ground that have been disturbed. Be considerate of other visitors by not spoiling their visual appreciation of natural habitats. And on private land, the obvious should always be understood: collecting plants is prohibited unless prior approval has been granted; practice the same thoughtful, careful collection techniques to disturb the ground and the plants as little as possible. Should you be granted the privilege of taking edible plants from private land, make a point of returning the property owner's gesture with a special favor.

Chapter 1

Introduction

NEARLY EVERYONE HAS EATEN A WILD EDIBLE PLANT. NATIVE FRUITS, such as huckleberries, serviceberries, and wild raspberries, are familiar to many of us. And all tame food plants that we enjoy have been derived from wild plant stock.

Some might say, "Why eat edible wild plants?" Foremost, it's fun to look for them and harvest them. During your searches you can supplement your diet while hiking or camping or at home. Knowing you can readily feed yourself from the outdoors will give you a good feeling of independence and self-reliance. You will find it interesting to taste these wild plant foods and compare the tastes with those of cultivated plants. As you learn where to find these plants, you will gain a special appreciation and knowledge of your natural surroundings. You will become aware of wanting to preserve natural habitats where useful edible plants live. An added bonus to foraging edible wild plants is that we gain useful therapy for our hustle-bustle lives, in an outdoor form.

As your wild plant knowledge grows, pass it on, especially to young folks. This ensures that a love and appreciation of nature will continue into succeeding generations.

PRECAUTIONS

Approach the identification of plants covered in this book with a discriminating eye. Scrutinize the photographs, and try to evaluate all the key features. Bear in mind that plants that have obvious flowers are easiest to identify when they are in the flowering stage. If you have questions about an uncertain plant, leave it alone.

If you are lost, though, unable to find plants described in this book, and wish to try unknown plants on your own, be cautious. First learn to recognize several poisonous plants. I've covered nine of the common tempting, but poisonous, plants or plant groups in chapter 10. Don't rely on animals to test foods for you. A bird or mammal may suffer no ill effects from a food that could devastate you. These precautions will also keep you safer:

1. Avoid any plant that resembles parsley or wild carrot unless you are sure of its identity. The deadly water hemlock may be confused with the edible water parsnip or wild parsnip (see page 95).

2. Avoid all mushrooms unless you are certain of their identity. Several poisonous amanita mushrooms may be confused with the highly edible white lepiota mushroom.

3. Avoid white or red berries unless you are sure of the plant that bears them. Be especially aware of the toxic white or red fruits of baneberries (see page 89).

4. Avoid eating a plant in its youngest stage unless you are sure of its identity. Before flowers appear, bulbs of poisonous death camas can be confused with those of eminently edible camas (see page 92) and wild onion (see page 37).

Another precaution: harvest known wild plants only in places where you do not suspect spraying by herbicides and insecticides. Remember that fields of crop plants and roadsides are most likely to be sprayed. In an emergency, wash the desired plant parts well and assume that the plant has absorbed little of the chemicals.

In like manner, question water purity when pursuing such shore plants as cattails, bulrushes, and watercress (see chapter 6). If oily sheens are obvious or you have other reason to be suspicious of water in which these useful plants grow, forgo them for another place, another time. Parts of shore plants growing well above suspected water, on the other hand, may be quite safe. See chapter 11, Finding Water, for general information on natural indicators of water and sources of water.

PREPARATIONS

When you attempt to eat a wild plant, first prepare your mind. Don't expect a wild food to taste like a familiar tame food. Under emergency conditions, for sure, this taste similarity doesn't really matter. You're interested only in nourishment. But if a taste is pleasant and familiar, you've gained a bonus. Think of this: if you had never tasted coffee, would you savor the first mouthful or spit out the bitter-tasting fluid?

Parts of a plant must be eaten during the *right season* to be most palatable or flavorful. You wouldn't harvest corn on the cob after the husk had dried on the stalk or string beans after they had become tough and stringy. In each chapter you'll find a table with plants arranged according to season of use.

Devote time to trials with wild edible plants. Attempt to recognize the plants covered in this book within your area or as you travel. Begin with universally familiar dandelions and cattails and gradually develop your repertoire of less well-known foodstuffs. You will gain comfort in knowing you can rely on your "friends," especially as your list grows.

Once you identify a plant, watch for changes with the season so you can recognize it not only when the plant flowers but also in its early stages, when it matures, and when it dies back or becomes dormant in preparation for winter.

If you like roughing it, you might fashion a digging stick for extracting plant roots, tubers, and bulbs. Select a green stick, preferably of hardwood, an inch or more across. Peel away the bark. Shape the thicker end into a chisel point. Harden the stick by "baking"—but not scorching—in a campfire until the sap is driven out. Sharpen the chisel point by rubbing it on a rock, preferably of sandstone. Press the chisel end alongside a plant—easiest if the soil is moist—and lever out the root, tuber, or bulb. The digging stick may be 3 or 4 feet (0.9 to 1.2 m) long, or longer should you wish it to double as a hiking staff. If also used as a hiking staff, keep the chisel point uppermost to reduce the need for frequent sharpening. You may also use the digging stick or hiking staff to test snake-prone places, and as a protective tool against larger predatory animals or smaller rabid animals.

HOW TO USE THIS BOOK

This book includes fifty edible plants and seaweeds found in the U.S. and Canada. They were selected for their ease of identification, widespread occurrence, and having more than one use or being usable during more than one season of the year (edible plants not included in this book are those that can easily be confused with inedible varieties, for example, mushrooms, wild parsnips, wild carrots, and water parsnips). Each plant is illustrated by one or more photographs.

In the chapters that follow, plants are arranged first by general habitat. You should be able to identify the general habitat in which you find yourself. The major habitats covered are forests, grasslands, deserts, tundras, freshwater shores (lake, pond, or stream edges), and seacoasts. These habitats are characterized in chapters 2 through 7. Bear in mind that a plant may be found in more than a single habitat. And, in some cases, several. So, burdocks are placed with the forest plants, but they may also be found in thickets, waste places, fields, and along roadsides.

Plants are arranged secondarily by growth form: trees, shrubs, forbs, grasslike plants, lichens, and seaweeds. **Trees** are woody plants, at least 15 feet (4.6 m) tall, with a single stem or trunk. **Shrubs** are smaller than trees, with several stems arising from a clump. **Forbs** are nonwoody, broad-leaved plants, such as strawberries. **Grasslike plants** include grasses and their look-alikes, such as rushes, wild onions, and similar plants. Grasses are nonwoody, slender-leaved plants with usually hollow, jointed stems. (Forbs and grasses may be grouped together as herbs.) **Lichens** are special plants made up of fungi (like mushrooms) or algae that live intimately together and don't look like either fungi or algae living separately. Most lichens are crustlike, leaflike, or hairlike and often grow on trees, dead wood, rocks, and soil. **Seaweeds** are red, brown, or green algae that are generally attached to the sea bottom, rocks, or other solid objects by rootlike, anchoring devices called **holdfasts**. These plantlike organisms possess stemlike stalks and fronds, which may be flat and unbranched, branched, or threadlike, and sometimes may have air bladders for buoyancy.

Within each growth form, plants are arranged alphabetically by the common name, with the scientific name included within parentheses. An equal sign between names indicates additional terms for the same species. Keep in mind that a plant may have several common names but only a single scientific name. Shrubs of *Amelanchier* species, with highly edible berries, are also known as serviceberries, juneberries, sarviceberries, saskatoons, shadblows, and shadberries.

For each plant the key identifying features are supplied, along with one or more photographs. I've kept the botanical jargon to a minimum. Season and use follows, as well as comments on where the plant may be found.

Check chapter 9 for insight into the nutritional value of edible wild plants. And look over the selected plants in chapter 8 that have uses other than for food.

Become well acquainted with the nine common poisonous plants given in chapter 10. Get to know them during all seasons, not just when they flower.

Peruse chapter 11 for the vital need of water in emergencies, how to find it, and how to treat water of questionable purity. We take the availability of this commodity much too lightly. To perceive this better, embark on a winter camping trip and take note of the time spent in melting snow and ice to quench thirst and prevent dehydration.

EDIBLE PLANTS ARRANGED BY SEASON

In chapters 2 through 7, wild edible plants are arranged first by main habitats and second by growth form. Each of those chapters contains tables that arrange those same plants and their edible parts according to their uses through the four seasons. The tables help you quickly find useful plants during a particular season.

Bear in mind that the seasons during which edible plants blossom or develop for their edible use may vary considerably, depending mainly on elevation and latitude. (This point was driven home to me years ago when I witnessed the first pasqueflowers blossoming in mid-April in northwestern Minnesota at an elevation of about 1,000 feet, or 300 meters. Almost exactly two months later, in the Bighorn Mountains of north-central Wyoming, I saw blossoming pasqueflowers once again at 9,600 feet, or 2,900 meters!) On average, in the Rocky Mountains, temperature falls 3 to 4 degrees Fahrenheit and precipitation increases 4 to 5 inches (100 to 130 mm) for each 1,000-foot (305 m) increase in elevation. Each 1,000-foot rise in elevation corresponds to a 200-mile (320 km) trip northward. Plant development also varies with the direction of exposure to sunlight, especially northward versus southward exposure, amount of moisture, and soil type. Seasons for plant use in chapters 2 to 7 are probably most reliable for the region between 40 and 50 degrees north latitude without making allowances for differences in elevation.

The tables reveal that several wild plant foods are available even in winter. In the more northern regions, covered by snow and ice throughout the wintry season, possibilities include rose hips, hawthorn berries, basswood leaf buds, and the inner bark of pines and maples. Farther south, where snow accumulates sporadically or lasts only several days at a time, more plants become available. Among them are dock leaves, dandelion and thistle roots, wild onion bulbs, agaves, Mormon teas, watercress, and seaweeds.

*　　*　　*

A few conventions: The relatively few technical terms are **boldfaced** where first mentioned and explained. Common names of plants given here are those used most often; in some cases, several names have been assigned to a single plant or plant group. The included scientific name always specifies the plant or plant group should you be confused by the common names. Where words are unfamiliar, I provide informal pronunciations with the stressed syllables in capitals. As an example, my difficult-to-pronounce surname, Cvancara, is spoken *SWUHN-shuh-ruh*.

Chapter 2

Forests

FORESTS INCLUDE BOTH EVERGREEN AND DECIDUOUS FORESTS OR a mixture of the two. Evergreen forests vary, from dense lodgepole pine stands in much of the mountainous West and the eastern white pine of the northeastern U.S. to the somewhat scattered piñon pine–juniper woodlands of the American Southwest, often with open areas of shrub grassland or shrub land. Deciduous forests include maple and oak-hickory forests of the East and aspen-birch forests of the East and West. Some forest habitats are restricted to ravines, canyons, and streams or are reduced to thickets.

Flowers project from winged flower stalk. Leaf is 6¼ inches (159 mm) long.

KEY FEATURES Deciduous trees with heart-shaped leaves with sawtooth edges. Flowers are in yellowish or cream-colored clusters and hang from winged stalks. Leaf buds are usually red and alternate on twigs.

SEASON AND USE *SPRING:* **Young leaves**, raw in salads.

SUMMER: **Flowers** and **new seeds**, raw. Steep **flowers** in boiling water for a pleasant tea.

FALL–SPRING: **Leaf buds**, raw; slightly gummy.

WHERE FOUND Moist woods. Eastern U.S. and south-central and southeastern Canada.

MAPLES (*Acer* species)

① Lower maple leaf, hanging beneath winged seeds, is 10½ inches (267 mm) across; leaves of most maples are smaller than this one. ② Box elder is a member of the maple family whose leaves are made up of separate leaflets: a pair of winged seeds is 1⅛ inches (28 mm) across.

KEY FEATURES Deciduous trees with winged seeds in pairs. Most leaves are single with three to five pointed lobes except for box elder (*Acer negundo*), which has leaves of several leaflets; leaves usually have coarse, sawtooth edges. Leaf buds are opposite one another on the twigs.

SEASON AND USE *ALL YEAR:* **Inner bark**. Remove the outer bark (do not girdle the tree, which will kill it) and scrape or peel the thin, slimy layer from between the outer bark and the wood. Pound into a pulp and eat raw or cooked (boiled).

   LATE WINTER–EARLY SPRING: On warm days with frosty nights before the leaves appear, look for opposite buds to help identify. Break or cut small branches (only in an emergency) to induce dripping of the slightly sweet, watery sap; drink. A better method is to drill or cut an upward-slanting shallow hole on the sunny side of a trunk a few feet above the ground. Insert a plastic or metal tube or a short piece of a hollow stem from reed grass (page 63). Hang a container below to catch the dripping **sap**. The making of syrup requires much sap and much boiling: the ratio of syrup to sap is no better than about 1 to 40! The sap can also be concentrated by freezing and partially rethawing to remove the ice, which is almost pure water, and repeating the process several times. **Buds** or **newly opened leaves** can be a trailside nibble or added to salads.

WHERE FOUND Mainly moist woods. All of U.S., including Alaska, and much of temperate Canada.

 **OAKS** (*Quercus* species)

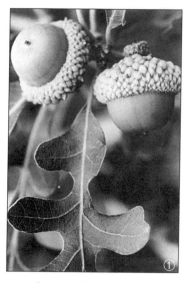

① Acorns of this member of the white oak group, including caps, are 1 inch (25 mm) across; leaf lobes are rounded. ② The grouped acorns are of a different oak and reveal the thin shell and the suggestion of worm attack (hole in one acorn).

KEY FEATURES Mostly deciduous trees or shrubs with **acorns**, egg-shaped or rounded nuts that fit into cuplike caps. Two groups: white oaks, usually with rounded-lobed leaves and acorns that aren't bitter, and red oaks, usually with pointed-lobed leaves and bitter acorns.

SEASON AND USE *FALL:* **Acorns**, raw or cooked (roasted). Remove any bitterness by soaking chopped or ground acorns in cold water or boiling them until the water is no longer brown. The bitterness is caused by tannins, which can be harmful if not removed. With a food grinder or two stones, grind roasted acorns into a meal for an instant coffee-like drink. Can also be used for cooked mush, to mix with wheat flour for baking, or to thicken soups. Rich in protein and fat.

WHERE FOUND Both wet and dry habitats. Conterminous U.S. and southernmost Canada.

FORESTS / OAKS

PINES (*Pinus* species)

① Pine needles partly obscure three green cones; the cone in the lower left corner is 3 inches (76 mm) long. ② The opened cone of piñon pine, 1³/₄ inches (44 mm) across, reveals the shells of six pine nuts. ③ Shells from another pine, cracked open; the longest pine nut measures 1³/₁₆ inches (30 mm) across.

KEY FEATURES Evergreen trees with needlelike leaves nearly always in bundles of two to five. Seeds, with or without wings, are in cones with or without prickles.

SEASON AND USE Other evergreen trees may be eaten in some of the same ways as pines. Firs and hemlocks have flat, blunt-tipped needles that are not in clusters; eat the inner bark and make tea from the needles. (The North American trees known as "hemlock" are un-related to the poisonous herbs known by the same name.) Spruces have four-sided, sharply pointed needles not in clusters; eat the inner bark.

ALL YEAR: **Inner bark**. Remove the outer bark, scrape or peel the thin, white, slimy layer from between the outer bark and the wood. Pound into a pulp and eat raw or cooked (boiled). May be resin fla-vored and fibrous but nutritious. Tea can be made from **needles**, which are rich in vitamins A and C. Cut away any resin from the needles. Try boiling a small handful of needles in 3 cups (700 mL) water. Tea from ponderosa pine (*Pinus ponderosa*) of the West is especially good.

SPRING: Soft center of **green cones**, cooked (boiled or roasted). May not be appealing. **Pollen**, rich in protein, is added to flour or can thick-en soups.

(continued next page)

FALL–EARLY WINTER: **Seeds** from cones, raw or cooked (roasted). Can be ground into meal and cooked into gruel or added to soups. Use especially the larger seeds of piñon pines (*P. edulis, P. monophylla,* and *P. quadrifolia*) and the digger pine (*P. sabiniana*), all in the southwestern U.S.; tasty.

OTHER USES Use pine pitch (as well as the pitch of other evergreens) for glue, especially when heated. Use the scaly, dry bark for fire starting.

WHERE FOUND Most of U.S., including Alaska, and much of temperate Canada.

SHRUBS
BLUEBERRIES, HUCKLEBERRIES, and DEERBERRIES

(*Vaccinium* species and *Gaylussacia* species)

These huckleberries are ³/₈ inch (10 mm) across.

KEY FEATURES Variable group of usually low deciduous shrubs**.** Berries are blue, black, or purple, with or without tufts at the unattached ends; with many soft seeds (*Vaccinium* spp.) or hard, seedlike nutlets (*Gaylussacia* spp.). Flowers are small, often urn shaped, and are white, pink, green, or purple. Leaves are egg shaped or elliptical, with sawtooth edges or not. **CAUTION:** Don't confuse with buckthorns, several species of which bear bitter, black to reddish, poisonous berries and may or may not have thorns. Berries contain two to four seedlike nutlets.

SEASON AND USE *SPRING–FALL:* Steep **leaves** in boiling water for tea; some kinds are better flavored than others.

SUMMER–FALL: Tasty, sweet **berries**, raw or cooked (boiled for soup).

WHERE FOUND Woods, woods openings, thickets, bogs, and tundras. Much of U.S., including Alaska, and most of temperate Canada.

CHOKECHERRY *(Prunus virginiana = P. melanocarpa)*

① Flower cluster is 3 inches (76 mm) long, and ② the largest berries are ³⁄₈ inch (10 mm) across.

KEY FEATURES A deciduous shrub or small tree. Berries are pea size, in long clusters, and are red, purple, or black, with hard, round, single pits. Leaves are egg shaped and pointed, with fine, sawtooth edges. Flowers are small; in long, bottlebrush-like clusters; and white.

SEASON AND USE *ALL YEAR:* Steep the **bark** in boiling water for tea. Try the tea for relief from abdominal cramps and diarrhea.

SUMMER–FALL: **Berries,** raw or cooked (boiled for soup); puckering or "choking" effect is dispelled upon cooking. **CAUTION:** Avoid berry pits, which contain cyanide.

WHERE FOUND Much of conterminous U.S. and most of temperate Canada.

CURRANTS and GOOSEBERRIES (*Ribes* species)

① Largest currant here is ³/₈ inch (10 mm) across. ② Prickly twig bears gooseberries up to ³/₈ inch (10 mm) across.

KEY FEATURES Low deciduous shrubs with small, often maplelike leaves with coarse, sawtooth edges. Flowers are white, yellow, pink, red, or purple. Berries are in clusters and are red, black, purple, yellow, or orange. Currants: Twigs usually have no prickles; berries are smooth skinned. Gooseberries: Twigs with prickles; berries are smooth skinned or prickly.

SEASON AND USE *SPRING:* Young **leaves**, cooked (steamed).
   SPRING–SUMMER: Sweet-tasting **flowers**, raw; some are better than others.
   SUMMER–FALL: **Berries,** raw or cooked (boiled); especially cook the prickly gooseberries.

WHERE FOUND Forests, thickets, swamps, fencerows, roadsides. Much of U.S., including Alaska, and much of temperate Canada.

FORESTS / CURRANTS AND GOOSEBERRIES

15

HAWTHORNS (= THORNAPPLES) (*Crataegus* species)

The largest berries here are $^1/_2$ inch (13 mm) across. The thorn to the right of the berries points downward.

KEY FEATURES Deciduous shrubs or small trees. Branches have long thorns. Fleshy fruits ("haws") resemble tiny apples with tufts at the unattached ends and are somewhat dry; are usually red or orange but also can be blue, black, or yellow; and have one to five seeds. Leaves have sawtooth edges and may be lobed. Flowers are white, pink, or red.

SEASON AND USE *FALL–WINTER:* **Fruit,** raw or cooked (into soup); spit out seeds. Fruit is somewhat dry. Pound the fruit, shape into patties, and dry in the sun for later use. Also steep the fruit in boiling water for tea; try adding a little wild mint (see page 57) if available.

OTHER USES Use the thorns as toothpicks and to help remove splinters, fine prickles, or bee stingers from the skin.

WHERE FOUND Wet or dry woods; also thickets, old fields, pastures. Much of U.S., including Alaska, and much of temperate Canada.

PLUMS (*Prunus* species)

The largest fruit here is $7/8$ inch (22 mm) across.

KEY FEATURES Deciduous shrubs or small trees; may have thorns. Fruit is round or egg shaped, up to 1 inch (25 mm) or more across; has a single, somewhat flattened pit; and is red, yellow, purple, or black. Leaves usually have sawtooth edges. Flowers are white.

SEASON AND USE *LATE SUMMER–FALL:* **Fruit**, raw or cooked (made into soup or sauce). Skin of the fruit may be sour.

WHERE FOUND Woods, thickets, draws, seashores (beach plum), fencerows, stream edges. Much of conterminous U.S. and south-central and southeastern Canada.

RASPBERRIES, BLACKBERRIES, THIMBLEBERRIES, SALMONBERRIES, and DEWBERRIES (*Rubus* species)

① Raspberry: largest berry is ¹/₂ inch (13 mm) across. ② Blackberry: flowers are 1¹/₈ inches (29 mm) across. Two Thimbleberries: ③ largest flowers are 1¹/₂ inches (38 mm) across and ④ largest berries are ⁵/₈ inch (16 mm) across.

KEY FEATURES Deciduous shrubs.

RASPBERRIES: Stems are arching, round, usually white powdered, and prickly. Berries are usually red, separate from a central plug. Leaves are usually divided into three to five leaflets; edges are sawtooth. Flowers are usually white.

BLACKBERRIES: Stems are arching or lying on the ground, angular, and prickly. Berries are black and do not separate from a central plug. Leaves and flowers are similar to those of raspberries.

THIMBLEBERRIES: Stems are like those of raspberries but are not prickly. Berries are like those of raspberries but drier. Leaves are maplelike. Flowers are usually white.

SALMONBERRIES: Stems are like those of raspberries but are not prickly. Berries are like those of raspberries but are yellow or red. Leaves are like those of raspberries. Flowers are reddish-purple. Pacific Coast.

DEWBERRIES: Flattened shrubs. Stems are round or angular, prickly, and lie on the ground. Berries are like those of blackberries. Leaves and flowers are similar to those of raspberries. Eastern North America.

Salmonberry: largest berry is about ³/₄ inch (19 mm) across.

SEASON AND USE *SPRING:* Peel the **young shoots** before any prickles harden; eat raw or cooked (boiled or steamed).

SUMMER: Steep the **leaves**, fresh (not wilted) or dried, in boiling water for tea; some kinds of raspberries and related plants are better for tea than others.

SUMMER–FALL: Tasty **berries**, raw or cooked (boiled).

WHERE FOUND Woods, thickets, roadsides, fields, meadows, swamps. Most of U.S., including Alaska, and most of Canada.

ROSES (*Rosa* species)

① Blossom is 2¼ inches (57 mm) across. ② Pendant hip is $^{3}/_{16}$ inch (5 mm) across—many hips are round, not elongate like this one.

KEY FEATURES Deciduous shrubs. Stems are prickly. Leaves are of three or more leaflets with sawtooth edges. Flowers are large and are pink, rose, or white. Fleshy fruits, called hips, are red or orange, dry, and have hairy seeds and tufts at the unattached ends.

SEASON AND USE *SPRING:* Young **shoots**, peeled and cooked (boiled).
   SUMMER: **Flower petals**, raw. Steep the young **leaves** in boiling water for tea.
   SUMMER–WINTER: Pulpy **hip** covering, raw or cooked (boiled into soup); remove the seeds first or spit them out later. Rich in vitamin C. Steep **whole hips** or just the **seeds** in boiling water for tea. **CAUTION:** Hairs on the seeds may irritate the intestine; strain the tea before drinking.

OTHER USES Apply moistened petals to minor wounds like Band-Aid bandages.

WHERE FOUND Woods, fields, swamps, fencerows, thickets, road-sides, bogs, prairies. Much of U.S., including Alaska, and much of temperate Canada.

FORESTS / ROSES

SERVICEBERRIES (= JUNEBERRIES = SARVICE-BERRIES = SASKATOONS = SHADBLOWS = SHADBERRIES) (*Amelanchier* species)

① Flower cluster is 1¹/₄ inches (32 mm) across, and ② largest dew-covered berries are ¹/₂ inch (13 mm) across.

KEY FEATURES Deciduous shrubs. Berries are purple-red to black with tufts at the unattached ends and have many small seeds. Leaves are egg shaped to round and sawtooth, at least away from the attached ends. Flowers are white or pink, clustered, have five petals, and often appear before the leaves. **CAUTION:** Similar to buckthorns, several species of which bear bitter, black to reddish, poisonous berries that lack tufts and may or may not have thorns. Berries contain two to four seedlike nutlets.

SEASON AND USE *SPRING–SUMMER:* Steep **young leaves** for tea.
SUMMER–FALL: Tasty **berries**, raw or cooked (boiled); some may be eaten green. May remain dried on bushes in winter.

WHERE FOUND Woods, thickets, stream banks, swamps, bogs. Much of U.S., including Alaska, and most of temperate Canada.

BURDOCKS (*Arctium* species)

① The largest of the rhubarblike leaves in the left center is 16½ inches (419 mm) long, and ② the flowers are ¾ inch (19 mm) across.

KEY FEATURES Burrs, which often stick to clothing, develop on stalks with purple to white flower heads. Leaves are large, egg shaped or heart shaped, and are woolly underneath; may resemble those of rhubarb. Up to 9 feet (2.7 m) tall, but often much less.

SEASON AND USE *Spring:* **Young leaves** and **leafstalks**, raw or cooked (boiled). Peel away the outer covering of leafstalks.

Summer: **Young flower stalks**, raw or cooked (boiled). Peel away the outer covering. May resemble a carrot in taste. **Taproots** of first-year plants (without flower stalks), cooked (boiled). Remove the thick rind from the core, which is cooked. Cut into small pieces. If bitter (as for leaves and leafstalks), change the cooking water one or more times. May be slightly stringy. May resemble string beans in flavor.

OTHER USES Use burrs like Velcro to fasten clothing. Wrap larger leaves around fish and meat for cooking in pits.

WHERE FOUND Woods, thickets, roadsides, waste places, fields. Much of conterminous U.S. and southern Canada.

SPRING BEAUTIES (*Claytonia* species)

① Flowers are ⁵/₈ inch (16 mm) across. ② Here two plants arise from a tuberlike corm that measures ⁷/₁₆ inch (11 mm) across.

KEY FEATURES Flowers are white or pink with darker pink veins. Leaves of most spring beauties are in a single, opposite pair; are elongated; and have smooth edges. Most have marble-size, round, tuberlike **corms** (unlike tubers, corms lack buds or eyes; they are not layered inside like bulbs) a few inches underground; alpine spring beauty has a thick, carrotlike taproot. Up to 12 inches (305 mm) high but often less.

SEASON AND USE *SPRING–SUMMER (DEPENDING ON ELEVATION):* **Tender leaves**, **stems**, and **flowers**, raw (in salad) or cooked (steamed or boiled). **Corms,** raw (radishlike flavor) or cooked (boiled or roasted; potato-like flavor). Dig only where plants are abundant.

WHERE FOUND Woods, thickets, high meadows, prairies, clearings, often near late snowbanks. Much of U.S., including Alaska, and much of temperate Canada.

 **STRAWBERRIES** (*Fragaria* species)

Largest berry is $^3/_8$ inch (10 mm) across, and largest flower is 1 inch (25 mm) across.

KEY FEATURES These low-to-ground plants resemble cultivated strawberries, but the fruit is smaller. Fruit has tiny seeds on the surface or embedded in pits. Leaves are of three coarsely sawtooth leaflets. Flowers are white or pink.

SEASON AND USE *SUMMER:* Tasty **berries**, raw or cooked (made into soup or sauce). Steep fresh (not wilted) or dried **leaves** for tea; rich in vitamin C. May add fruits to the tea.

WHERE FOUND Woods, fields, meadows, thickets, dunes (stable), and along streams. Much of U.S., including Alaska, and much of temperate Canada.

FOREST PLANTS BY SEASON

Plant or Plant Group	Parts Eaten

SPRING

TREES
Basswoods . . . . leaf buds, young leaves
Maples . . . . inner bark, sap, buds, and
newly opened leaves
Pines . . . . inner bark, needles (tea),
green cones, pollen

SHRUBS
Blueberries and similar plants . . . . leaves (tea)
Chokecherry . . . . bark (tea)
Currants and gooseberries . . . . young leaves, flowers
Raspberries and similar plants . . . . young shoots
Roses . . . . young shoots
Serviceberries . . . . young leaves (tea)

FORBS
Burdocks . . . . young leaves, leafstalks
Springbeauties . . . . corms or taproots; young leaves,
stems, and flowers

SUMMER

TREES
Basswoods . . . . flowers, new seeds
Maples . . . . inner bark
Pines . . . . inner bark, needles (tea)

SHRUBS
Blueberries and similar plants . . . . leaves (tea), berries
Chokecherry . . . . bark (tea), berries
Currants and gooseberries . . . . flowers, berries
Plums . . . . fruit
Raspberries and similar plants . . . . leaves (tea), berries
Roses . . . . flower petals, leaves (tea),
seeds (tea), hips
Serviceberries . . . . young leaves (tea), berries

FORBS
Burdocks . . . . young flower stalks, taproots
Springbeauties . . . . corms or taproots, young leaves
and stems
Strawberries . . . . berries, leaves (tea)

(continued next page)

FOREST PLANTS BY SEASON

25

Plant or Plant Group	Parts Eaten

FALL

TREES

Basswoods.	leaf buds
Maples	inner bark
Oaks.	acorns
Pines	inner bark, needles (tea), pine nuts

SHRUBS

Blueberries and similar plants.	leaves (tea), berries
Chokecherry.	bark (tea), berries
Currants and gooseberries.	berries
Hawthorns	berries
Plums.	fruit
Raspberries and similar plants	berries
Roses	hips, seeds (tea)
Serviceberries.	berries

WINTER

TREES

Basswoods.	leaf buds
Maples	inner bark, sap (late winter), buds
Pines	inner bark, needles (tea), pine nuts (early winter)

SHRUBS

Chokecherry.	bark (tea)
Hawthorns	berries
Roses	hips, seeds (tea)

Chapter 3

Grasslands

GRASSLANDS INCLUDE PRAIRIES, MEADOWS, AND SHRUB OR tree grasslands. The North American prairie once extended from the Rocky Mountains to the forests of the East and into south-central Canada. Only remnants now exist, but they can be found in many places. Meadows are smaller grasslands, are wet or dry, and exist at low or high elevations. Some grasslands contain scattered shrubs or trees, such as sagebrush grasslands and oak savannas.

Grasses dominate, but forbs are conspicuous. Shrubs and trees, if not scattered as mentioned, nearly always occur along streams, ponds, and lakes and often in ravines and thickets.

For the purposes of this book, I've included human-created habitats of disturbed ground—such as fields, gardens, road ditches, pastures, and waste places—within the general habitat of grasslands. In these expect such adaptable edibles as dandelions, docks, lamb's-quarters, and milkweeds.

COMMON DANDELION (*Taraxacum officinale*)

This root is 9½ inches (241 mm) long.

KEY FEATURES A familiar lawn weed with milky sap. Leaves are clustered at ground level and have sharp lobes. Flowers are one to a stalk, yellow, and are replaced by white seed balls. Up to 2 feet (0.6 m) tall but usually less. Plant is rich in vitamins A and C.

SEASON AND USE *SPRING–SUMMER:* **Young leaves**, before flowers show, raw (in salad) or cooked (steamed or boiled); older leaves may be bitter. **Crown** of white leaf bases at top of root, raw or cooked (boiled). **Young flower buds** within crown while they still hang down, raw or cooked (boiled). **Flowers**, raw in salads or cooked (boiled). Try a tea from flower buds and flowers. When eating buds or flowers, avoid the bitter stem.

    ALL YEAR: **Roots**, which are easier to dig when ground is wet; peeled, cut into pieces, raw or cooked (boiled). If edible parts are bitter when cooked, change the water one or more times. For a coffeelike drink, roast the **roots** until they break with a snap. Grind with a food grinder or two stones and boil or steep.

OTHER USES Milky sap can be used as an emergency glue.

WHERE FOUND Grasslands, fields, gardens, roadsides, thickets, open woods. Most of U.S., including Alaska, and most of temperate Canada.

DOCKS
(*Rumex* species, especially *R. crispus* and similar species)

The height of the seed stalk in the foreground is 41 inches (1 m).

KEY FEATURES Leaves are mostly in a rosette at the base of the plant and are mostly lance shaped, oblong, and egg shaped. Flowers are greenish, in spikelike clusters; they develop into tiny, reddish-brown, three-sided seeds, usually with three wings. Up to 6 feet (1.8 m) tall but often less.

SEASON AND USE *SPRING:* Tender **young leaves**, raw in salads or cooked (steamed or boiled). If bitter, change the cooking water one or more times. May combine with dandelion leaves or buds. Rich in vitamins A and C.

SUMMER: **Young green seeds**, boiled, or added to soups.

FALL–WINTER: Gather second crop of **young leaves**; eat as in the spring. Collect **seeds** from reddish-brown clusters (may project above snow). Try to separate the seeds from the winged hulls by rubbing them between the hands or two stones. Grind seeds with a food grinder or two stones and cook into gruel. CAUTION: Avoid eating the roots, which are high in tannic acid.

WHERE FOUND Grasslands, roadsides, ditches, fields, waste places, wet ground, thickets, pastures, shores. Most of U.S., including Alaska, and most of Canada to the Arctic.

YELLOW EVENING PRIMROSE (*Oenothera biennis*)

The uppermost blossom is 1¹/₈ inches (28 mm) across.

KEY FEATURES Flowers are yellow, have four petals, and often fade to pink or purple; upper part of the pistil (most central seed-bearing part of flower) is X-shaped; leafy **sepals**, just beneath petals, are bent downward. Seedpods are cylinder shaped. Leaves of the first-year plant (without flower stalk) are elongate, in a rosette at ground level; those of the second-year plant are lance shaped and mostly without leaf-stalks, on a tall flower stalk. Up to 6 feet (1.8 m) tall. Other evening primroses are also edible; some have white and pink flowers.

SEASON AND USE *FALL–SPRING:* Reddish **young leaves** of first-year plants, raw or cooked (boiled or steamed).

SUMMER: **Flower buds** and **flowers**, raw or cooked (boiled). **Petals** as salad garnishes. Twist off **young seedpods**, raw or cooked (boiled). Sprinkle **seeds** on salads.

ALL YEAR (BEST, FALL–SPRING): **Roots**, best of the first-year plants, cooked (boiled). Change the cooking water of leaves, seedpods, and roots one or more times to remove any bitter taste.

WHERE FOUND Grasslands, roadsides, waste places, fencerows, stream banks. Most of conterminous U.S. and southern Canada.

GRASSLANDS / YELLOW EVENING PRIMROSE

INDIAN BREADROOT (= PRAIRIE TURNIP = TIPSIN = COMMON BREADROOT)
(*Psoralea esculenta* and similar species)

The ruler is 6 inches (152 mm) long.

KEY FEATURES Plant is mostly covered with hairs. Leaves are comprised of three to five elongate leaflets. Pea-shaped flowers are bluish, are in oblong spikes, and are replaced by tiny seedpods. Turnip-shaped roots are a few inches underground. Up to $1^1/_2$ feet (400 mm) high.

SEASON AND USE *SPRING–SUMMER:* Peeled **roots**, raw or cooked (boiled or roasted), or dried for later use. They resemble a nutty potato and are rich in starch and sugar. Dig the root before the upper part of the perennial plant dies and separates from the root. Dried roots can be ground into a meal for thickening soups or cooked into a gruel.

WHERE FOUND Mostly prairies. Great Plains south to Texas; west to Colorado, New Mexico, Arizona, Utah, and California; and south-central Canada.

LAMB'S-QUARTERS (*Chenopodium album* and similar species)

The large leaf at upper left is 3¹/₈ inches (79 mm) long.

KEY FEATURES A weed, the leaves of which are coated with a water-resistant, white, mealy covering, especially on the undersides. Lower leaves are diamond shaped, arrowhead shaped, or egg shaped and sawtooth; upper leaves are narrow, often with smooth edges. Flowers are tiny, in greenish or reddish clusters. Seeds are tiny, black, shiny. Up to 6 feet (1.8 m) tall but usually 1 to 3 feet (0.3 to 0.9 m). **CAUTION:** Similar to Mexican Tea, which smells of varnish, is not mealy, and is edible only when dried.

SEASON AND USE *SPRING–FALL:* **Young upper leaves**; eat raw in salads or steam or boil until they are easily cut by a spoon or a flat stick. **Flowers**, eat raw or cooked (boiled). Strip off **green seeds**, add to salads and soups. May combine with dock greens. One of the best potherbs; resembles rough-textured spinach. High in protein, calcium, and vitamins A and C.

   FALL–EARLY WINTER: Strip off the **ripe seeds**, grind with a food grinder or two stones, and cook into a gruel or mix with flour for baking.

WHERE FOUND Occupies grassland or what was once grassland; is most common in disturbed, waste, and cultivated ground. Most of U.S., including Alaska, and much of temperate Canada.

 **MILKWEEDS** (*Asclepias* species)

The blossoms here are up to $^{11}/_{16}$ inch (17 mm) across.

KEY FEATURES Plants mostly with a milky sap, hairy or not. Leaves are mostly lance shaped, egg shaped, oblong, or ellipse shaped. Flowers are arranged in domed clusters and are white, pink, red, purple, green, yellow, or orange; lower five parts of each flower are bent backward. Seedpods are pointed and are warty or spiny. Up to 6 feet (1.8 m) tall but often less. **CAUTION**: Avoid Butterfly Weed, a poisonous, orange-flowered milkweed that lacks milky sap. To be safe, don't eat any milkweeds in large quantities.

SEASON AND USE *SPRING*: **Young top leaves**. Boil, changing the water at least once to remove the bitterness of the milky sap, which may be harmful. Narrow-leaved milkweeds may be more harmful than broad-leaved milkweeds. (Young shoots are also edible but may be confused with the young shoots of poisonous dogbanes, also with a milky sap.)

SUMMER: **Flower buds, flowers**, and **young seedpods**. Gather the buds while they are young and green and the seedpods while they are tender and firm. Boil in water, changing the water one or more times. Pick the upper parts of the flowers and eat cooked (boiled).

OTHER USES Dry **down** of seedpods can be used for tinder to start campfires or as insulation for boots. Milky sap can be used as a glue.

WHERE FOUND Grasslands, fields, roadsides, open woods, pastures, fencerows, waste places, ditches, bogs, thickets, swamps, and marshes. Much of conterminous U.S. and southern Canada.

GRASSLANDS / MILKWEEDS

COMMON SUNFLOWER (*Helianthus annuus*)

This blossom is
3⁷/₈ inches
(98 mm) across.

KEY FEATURES Flower heads are up to 5 inches (127 mm) across and are brownish in the center and yellow around the outside. Stems and leaves are rough and hairy. Leaves are heart shaped or spade shaped; the lowest leaves are opposite one another and the upper leaves alternate with one another. Up to 10 feet (3 m) tall.

SEASON AND USE *SUMMER:* **Flower buds**, cooked (boiled); may need to change the cooking water to avoid bitterness. Yellow **outside** part of the **flower head**, raw.

SUMMER–FALL: **Seeds**, raw or roasted, best with the hulls removed. Seeds can also be roasted, ground, and boiled for a coffeelike drink.

WHERE FOUND Grasslands, waste places, fields, roadsides, along railroad tracks. Most of U.S., including Alaska, and much of temperate Canada.

 **THISTLES** (*Cirsium* species)

This blossom is 2 inches (50 mm) across.

KEY FEATURES Leaves are prickly, with deep cuts. Stems are not winged by the bases of the leaves. Flowers are of a "shaving brush" style and are white, red, or purple. Up to at least 6 feet (1.8 m) tall.

SEASON AND USE *Spring:* **Young leaves**, raw or cooked (steamed or boiled). First remove the prickles.

Spring–Summer: **Young stems** and **flower stalks**, raw or cooked (steamed or boiled). Peel for the inner, pithy part.

Fall–Spring: **Roots** of first-year plants (those with leaves but without stems), raw or cooked (boiled or roasted). The root of the elk thistle (*Cirsium foliosum*) of the West is well confirmed as a survival food.

OTHER USES **Thistledown** (fluff clinging to seeds) of some thistles can be used as tinder to start a campfire. Chew water-rich stalks to quench thirst.

WHERE FOUND Grasslands, pastures, roadsides, woods, thickets, fields, shores, dunes, bogs, and swamps. Much of U.S., including Alaska, and much of temperate Canada.

CAMAS (= CAMASS = BLUE CAMAS)
(*Camassia quamash* and others)

① This flower cluster is 9½ inches (241 mm) high. ② The largest bulb, 1¼ inches (32 mm) across, was found 6 inches (152 mm) below the base of the plant.

KEY FEATURES Flowers are blue or purplish, sometimes white, and are arranged in elongate clusters. Leaves are grasslike at the base of the stem. Underground bulb is onionlike but odorless. Between 1 and 2 feet (0.3 to 0.6 m) high. **CAUTION**: Similar to poisonous death camas, which has a similar bulb but with cream-colored or white flowers and V-creased leaves (V-shaped where cut across).

SEASON AND USE *ALL YEAR*, but best dug in *SPRING–SUMMER*, when plants are in flower (see CAUTION above): **Bulbs**, raw or cooked (boiled or roasted), or dried for later use; slightly slimy; rich in sugar.

WHERE FOUND Western species are mostly found in moist meadows and along streams; British Columbia and Alberta to California and east to Utah, Montana, and Wyoming. An eastern U.S. and Ontario species grows in meadows, moist open woods, and fields.

ONIONS, GARLICS, AND LEEKS (*Allium* species)

This onion flower cluster is 1³/₄ inches (44 mm) across.

KEY FEATURES Leaves are flat to round (where cut across), usually grasslike, and arise from the base of the plant. Tiny flowers are at the top of the stalk in a rounded cluster and are white, yellow, pink, red, or purple. The leaves and the underground bulb have an onionlike odor. Up to 3 feet (0.9 m) tall. Rich in vitamins C and A. **CAUTION**: Similar to death camas, which has a similar bulb, lacks the onionlike odor, and has V-creased leaves (V-shaped where cut across).

SEASON AND USE *ALL YEAR:* **Bulbs**, raw or cooked (boiled or steamed), or dried for later use. Can be eaten as the primary part of a meal or used to flavor other foods, especially soups and stews.

SPRING–FALL: **Leaves**, raw or cooked (boiled or steamed). Can be eaten as the primary part of a meal or used to flavor other foods. Both bulbs and leaves are high in vitamins C and A.

OTHER USES Rub the juice from bruised leaves or bulbs on the body as an insect repellent or to relieve itching from insect bites. Try the juice for coughs or colds.

WHERE FOUND Grasslands, thickets, woods, pastures, fields, roadsides, and shores. Most of U.S., including Alaska, and much of temperate Canada.

SALSIFIES (= GOAT'S-BEARDS = OYSTER PLANTS)
(*Tragopogon* species)

The seed ball is
4¹/₄ inches
(108 mm) across.

KEY FEATURES Weeds with a milky sap. Leaves are grasslike and clasp the smooth stem. Flowers have single heads, are yellow or purple, and are replaced by seed balls much larger than those of dandelions. Up to 3 feet (0.9 m) or more tall.

SEASON AND USE *SPRING:* **Young leaves** and **crowns** (clusters of leaf bases just above roots), raw or cooked (boiled or steamed). **Flower buds** and **flowers** in salads.

ALL YEAR (BEST FALL–SPRING): First-year (without a flower stalk) **roots**, raw or cooked (boiled or roasted); first peel the roots. May taste like parsnips or oysters; spit out any fibers. If you boil the leaves or roots, change the cooking water one or more times to remove any bitter taste.

WHERE FOUND Grasslands, fields, gardens, waste places, roadsides, pastures, and fencerows. Most of conterminous U.S. and southern Canada.

Plant or Plant Group   **Parts Eaten**

SPRING

FORBS

Common Dandelion . . . . young leaves, crown,
flower buds, flowers,
roots (also coffee substitute)

Docks . . . . young leaves

Yellow Evening Primrose . . . . young leaves, roots

Indian Breadroot . . . . root

Lamb's-quarters . . . . young leaves, flowers,
green seeds

Milkweeds . . . . young leaves

Thistles . . . . young leaves, stems,
flower stalks, roots

GRASSLIKE PLANTS

Camas . . . . bulbs

Onions and similar plants . . . . leaves, bulbs

Salsifies . . . . young leaves, flower buds,
flowers, roots

SUMMER

FORBS

Common Dandelion . . . . young leaves, crown, flower
buds, roots (also coffee
subst.)

Docks . . . . young green seeds

Yellow Evening Primrose . . . . roots, flower buds, flowers,
seedpods, seeds

Indian Breadroot . . . . root

Lamb's-quarters . . . . young leaves, flowers,
green seeds

Milkweeds . . . . flower buds, flowers, young
seedpods

Common Sunflower . . . . flower buds, flowers (outer),
seeds (also coffee subst.)

Thistles . . . . young stems, flower stalks,
roots

GRASSLIKE PLANTS

Camas . . . . bulbs

Onions and similar plants . . . . leaves, bulbs

Salsifies . . . . roots

(continued next page)

Plant or Plant Group	Parts Eaten

FALL

FORBS

Common Dandelion. . . . . roots (also coffee subst.)

Docks. . . . . young leaves, seeds

Yellow Evening Primrose . . . . young leaves, roots

Lamb's-quarters . . . . young leaves, flowers, green and ripe seeds

Common Sunflower . . . . seeds (also coffee subst.)

Thistles. . . . . roots

GRASSLIKE PLANTS

Onions and similar plants . . . . leaves, bulbs

Salsifies . . . . roots

WINTER

FORBS

Common Dandelion. . . . . roots (also coffee subst.)

Docks. . . . . young leaves, seeds

Yellow Evening Primrose . . . . young leaves, roots

Lamb's-quarters . . . . ripe seeds

Thistles. . . . . roots

GRASSLIKE PLANTS

Onions and similar plants . . . . bulbs

Salsifies . . . . roots

Chapter 4

Deserts

DESERTS ARE DRY PLACES WITH LOW ANNUAL PRECIPITATION (less than 10 in. or 254 mm), high evaporation, and sparse vegetation. Contrary to what Hollywood frequently portrays, plant-free sand dunes are rare.

Deserts north of Mexico are concentrated in the American Southwest and adjacent regions: Nevada, southeastern and northeastern California, southeastern Oregon, southern Idaho, most of Utah, southwestern Wyoming, much of Arizona, southern and western Colorado, southern and northwestern New Mexico, and southwestern Texas.

Though sparse, plants in deserts are sufficient and varied. Trees are scarce. Some plants, notably yuccas and prickly pear cacti, may be found in drier grasslands as well as in deserts. Always be on the lookout for such wide-ranging possibilities.

Keep in mind that elevation plays a big role as to which plants are available in deserts. Even small mountains create forested havens in deserts. The Chiricahua Mountains in extreme southeastern Arizona constitute a sky island in a desert sea.

AGAVES (*uh-GAH-veez*) (= CENTURY PLANTS = MESCALS) (*Agave* species)

① Flower stalk, about 25 feet (7.6 m) tall, and rosettes of leaves. ② These agave leaves have prickly leaf edges; the tallest leaves here are 1$\frac{1}{2}$ feet (400 mm) high.

KEY FEATURES A rosette of thick, juicy, spikelike leaves at the base of the plant, whose edges tend to be prickly; leaves are similar to those of African aloes (*Ay-lowz*), which usually lack a stem; may resemble the leaves of some yuccas whose edges are not prickly. Flowers are red, yellow, purple, or green, on stalks up to 40 feet (12.2 m) tall; after flowering, the plant dies.

SEASON AND USE CAUTION: Some agaves are poisonous or irritating. Consult local wild edible plant experts for the clearly edible species of agaves.

SPRING: **Flower stalks**, when they barely arise from the rosette of leaves, cooked (boiled). **Flower buds** and **flowers**, cooked (boiled).

ALL YEAR (BUT BEST IN SPRING AND SUMMER): **Center** of the base of the plant, with leaf bases and the possible base of the flower stalk. Pry out this "butt" (or "heart" or "crown") of the plant with a spade or a stout chisel-pointed stick and roast in a fire pit or boil; if roasted, may have a smoky, datelike flavor. Spit out the fibers.

OTHER USES For a shelter's roof covering, lay the leaves like tiles.

WHERE FOUND Arizona, California, New Mexico, Texas, Utah.

CHOLLAS (*CHOY-yuhz*) (*Opuntia* species)

① This bush is 5¹/₂ feet (1.6 m) high. ② Fruits are 1¹/₂ to 1³/₄ inches (38 to 44 mm) long at tips of darker-colored branches.

KEY FEATURES Stem is cylinderlike, spiny, jointed, and resembles a stiff rope. Flowers are red, orange, yellow, or green. Fruits are dry, yellow, appear at the tips of branches, and have many small seeds. The dead stem is a woody, hollow cylinder with a lacy pattern. Up to 9 feet (2.7 m) tall.

SEASON AND USE *SPRING:* **Flower buds** and **young stem segments,** cooked (boiled or roasted). First burn or cut off the spines; be especially careful of the hairlike spines. Peel.

    SUMMER–SPRING: **Fruits,** raw or cooked (boiled or roasted). First remove any spines and seeds. May have a bland taste and are slightly slimy. The fruits can be dried for later use; before eating, soak until soft.

OTHER USES The dried wood can be used as campfire fuel.

WHERE FOUND Arizona, California, Colorado, Kansas, Nevada, New Mexico, Oklahoma, Texas, and Utah.

DESERTS / CHOLLAS

MORMON TEAS (= JOINTFIRS) (*Ephedra* species)

① This bush is 4 feet (1.2 m) tall. ② Twigs have tiny, scalelike leaves.

KEY FEATURES Often light green or yellow-green shrubs. Twigs are slender, stiff, and jointed and appear opposite each other or in whorls. Cores contain a reddish-brown powder. Leaves are tiny, scalelike, and are paired or in threes at the joints. Up to 4 feet (1.2 m) tall.

SEASON AND USE *ALL YEAR:* Place snapped **twigs** in boiling water and steep for tea. Experiment for tea strength. Tea is yellow or pink and pleasant tasting.

WHERE FOUND Deserts and other dry habitats. Drier regions of Arizona, California, Colorado, Idaho, Nevada, New Mexico, Oregon, Texas, Utah, and Wyoming.

FOUR-WING SALTBUSH (*Atriplex canescens*)

Leaves, up to ³/₄ inch (19 mm) long, and four-winged seeds.

KEY FEATURES Seeds have four wings at right angles to each other; may be in solid masses. Leaves are narrow, have smooth edges, and are covered with tiny silvery scales. Flowers are tiny, with yellow, gray, or green spikes. Up to 6 feet (1.8 m) tall.

SEASON AND USE *SPRING–FALL:* **Leaves**, raw or cooked (steamed). Salty.

WHERE FOUND Deserts, in semiarid habitats including shrub land, shrub grassland, and grassland. In areas with alkaline and nonalkaline soils. South Dakota to Washington and south to California and Texas.

YUCCAS (= SOAPWEEDS = SPANISH BAYONETS)
(Yucca species)

① This flower spike is 27 inches (686 mm) tall. ② Flowers and buds close-up. ③ The buds on these yucca bloom spikes are mostly not yet separated; The spike on the left is 14 inches (356 mm) tall.

KEY FEATURES Appear as shrubs or moderate-size trees (e.g., the Joshua tree). Leaves are daggerlike or swordlike, stiff, and often have curled threads at the edges; they cluster densely at the base of the plant or at the tips of the branches. Flowers are whitish, large, and appear in clusters. Oblong seedpods release black, flat seeds.

SEASON AND USE *SPRING–SUMMER:* **Young flower stalk** (when it emerges from the leaf cluster but before the buds expand), **flower buds** and **flowers**, and **young seedpods**; eat all raw or cooked (boiled or roasted). Flower stalk, buds, and flowers may taste like asparagus; seedpods may taste like peas. (May wish to peel young flower stalks and seedpods before eating.) Examine the flowers and seedpods for insect larvae. Some yuccas, especially the banana yucca, have fleshy, fruitlike seedpods. **CAUTION:** Don't eat raw yucca parts in large quantities; some of the contained substances may cause ill effects.

OTHER USES Soap from the **root,** which can be unearthed with a spade or a stout, chisel-pointed stick. Peel the outer layer and pound the root to a pulp. Shake in water for a lather. Try using a trimmed spiny **tip of a leaf, with an attached, central-most fiber,** like needle and thread to repair clothing. Pound the leaf to help separate the fibers.

WHERE FOUND Deserts, and also in other drier habitats, including old fields, dunes, and sand hills. Much of conterminous U.S. and part of southern Canada.

FORBS
PRICKLY PEAR CACTI (*Opuntia* species)

① The largest stem (with buds) is about 8 inches (203 mm) high. ② The largest fruit here is 2¹/₈ inches (54 mm) high. ③ This blossom is 3 inches (76 mm) across, with stem and buds.

KEY FEATURES Fleshy, jointed stems are covered with spines. Stems are often flattened but may be round where cut across. Flowers are yellow, red, orange, pink, or purple. Leaves are small and fleshy, drop off early, and appear with spine clusters. Up to 10 feet (3 m) tall but usually much less.

SEASON AND USE *SPRING–EARLY SUMMER:* **Young,** tender **stems,** raw or cooked (boiled or roasted); somewhat slimy, may taste like cucumber. (The older stems are also edible, but they are not as good.) First peel away or burn the spines; especially avoid the hairlike spines. Hairlike spines can also be removed with a damp cloth.

MIDSUMMER–FALL: Red, purple, tan, or yellowish fleshy **fruits,** raw or cooked (steamed). First peel away, burn, or whisk away the hairlike spines with a bunch of stiff grass; you may wish to remove the skin and seeds. Some fruits are dry.

OTHER USES Juicy **stems** can be a source of water, as with other cacti.

WHERE FOUND Deserts and other dry habitats. Much of conterminous U.S. and much of southern Canada.

DESERTS / PRICKLY PEAR CACTI

DESERT PLANTS BY SEASON

Plant or Plant Group	Parts Eaten

SPRING

SHRUBS

Agaves . . . . flower stalks, flower buds, flowers, "heart"

Chollas . . . . flower buds, young stems, fruits (old)

Mormon Teas . . . . twigs (tea)

Four-Wing Saltbush . . . . leaves

Yuccas . . . . young flower stalks, buds, flowers, young seedpods

FORBS

Prickly Pear Cacti . . . . young stems

SUMMER

SHRUBS

Agaves . . . . "heart"

Chollas . . . . fruits

Mormon Teas . . . . twigs (tea)

Four-Wing Saltbush . . . . leaves

Yuccas . . . . young flower stalks, flower buds, flowers, young seedpods

FORBS

Prickly Pear Cacti . . . . young stems, fruits

FALL

SHRUBS

Agaves . . . . "heart"

Chollas . . . . fruits

Mormon Teas . . . . twigs (tea)

Four-Wing Saltbush . . . . leaves

FORBS

Prickly Pear Cacti . . . . fruits

WINTER

SHRUBS

Agaves . . . . "heart"

Chollas . . . . fruits

Mormon Teas . . . . twigs (tea)

Chapter 5

Tundras

TUNDRAS ARE LEVEL OR ROLLING TERRAINS—TREELESS OR nearly so—in parts of Alaska and northern Canada (Arctic tundra), and in the high mountains above timberline (alpine tundra). In this habitat of permanently frozen subsoil, dominant plants include mosses, lichens, herbs, and small shrubs. Besides the plants included here, look for tundra counterparts of wild onions and thistles (see pages 37 and 35), spring beauty (with a thick, carrotlike taproot; see page 23), and yarrow (see page 79).

GLACIER LILY (= DOGTOOTH VIOLET = SNOW LILY) (*Erythronium grandiflorum*)

Upper blossom
is 1½ inches
(38 mm) across.

KEY FEATURES Nodding flowers are yellow and have six petals bent backward. Two lance-shaped leaves at the base of the plant have smooth edges. Underground bulb. Up to 12 inches (305 mm) tall but often less.

SEASON AND USE *SPRING:* **Leaves** as greens, raw or cooked (steamed).
SPRING–SUMMER: Green **seedpods** and **bulbs**, cooked (boiled). Collect the bulbs only where they are abundant to conserve the plants.
CAUTION: Eating bulbs may sometimes cause a burning sensation or other ill effects. If that happens, call the nearest Poison Control Center for aid.

WHERE FOUND Often at the edge of melting snow. Alpine tundra, at lower elevations in meadows, woods, and along stream banks. British Columbia and Alberta, south to Colorado and Utah, west to California.

ROSECROWN (*Sedum rhodanthum = Clementsia rhodantha = Rhodiola rhodantha*)

Whorl of leaves of largest plant is 1¼ inches (32 mm) across.

KEY FEATURES Leaves are fleshy, without leafstalks; are oblong or narrower; and have smooth or finely sawtooth margins. Flowers are rose, pink, or rarely white and appear in clusters at the tops of unbranched stems, somewhat similar to those of red clover. Up to 12 inches (305 mm) tall. A similar edible plant is Roseroot (*Rhodiola rosea = Sedum roseum = S. integrifolium*), which has dark red to purple or yellow flowers in shorter clusters and has broader (egg-shaped) leaves.

SEASON AND USE *SPRING–SUMMER:* **Leaves** and **shoots**, raw or cooked (steamed or boiled). **Roots,** cooked (boiled).

OTHER USES Chew the fleshy leaves as a source of water.

WHERE FOUND Moist meadows and along stream banks. Alaska, northwest Canada, British Columbia, Alberta, to Arizona and Colorado.

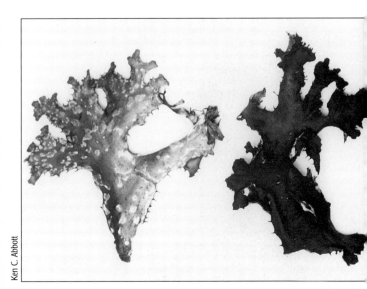

Ken C. Abbott

Underside (*left*) and upper surface (*right*). Each piece is about 1 inch (25 mm) high.

KEY FEATURES Leafy lichens that form green to brown mats. Upper and lower surfaces may be similarly or differently colored. Stems and branches are straplike, thin, and have tiny spines along their edges; flattened when wet, edges curl inward when dry. Up to 4 inches (101 mm) tall but often less.

SEASON AND USE *ALL YEAR:* Dry and grind the **entire plants** into a powder. Boil to a jellylike gruel. May add the powder to soups.
CAUTION: Plants contain acids that may upset the digestive system. Before drying, soak the plants or boil them in two or more changes of water to remove the acids.

OTHER USES Can be cooked as a gruel to relieve coughs and colds.

WHERE FOUND Alpine and Arctic tundra as well as lower elevations and farther south in mostly exposed areas; on soil and upper parts of logs. Arctic south to Washington, New Mexico, and southern Appalachian Mountains.

ROCK TRIPES (*Umbilicaria* species)

Upper (*top*) and lower (*bottom*) surfaces show near-central point of attachment. Upper lichen is 2 inches (50 mm) across.

KEY FEATURES Leafy lichens that are attached to rocks at their centers. Nearly circular, gray to brown above, darker below. Upper surface is smooth or has ridges or blisters. Leathery when wet, brittle when dry. Up to 10 inches (254 mm) across.

SEASON AND USE *ALL YEAR:* **Entire plant,** raw (in small amounts), better cooked (boiled). **CAUTION**: Plants contain acids that may upset the digestive system. Before eating raw or cooked, soak the plants, changing the water two or more times, to remove the acids.

WHERE FOUND Alpine and Arctic tundra as well as lower elevations and farther south in open or sheltered areas. Arctic south to California, Arizona, New Mexico, and southern Appalachian Mountains.

TUNDRA PLANTS BY SEASON

Plant or Plant Group	Parts Eaten

SPRING

FORBS
Glacier Lily . . . . leaves, seedpods, bulbs
Rosecrown . . . . leaves, shoots, roots

LICHENS
Iceland Mosses . . . . entire plants
Rock Tripes . . . . entire plants

SUMMER

FORBS
Glacier Lily . . . . seedpods, bulbs
Rosecrown . . . . leaves, shoots, roots

LICHENS
Iceland Mosses . . . . entire plants
Rock Tripes . . . . entire plants

FALL

LICHENS
Iceland Mosses . . . . entire plants
Rock Tripes . . . . entire plants

WINTER

LICHENS
Iceland Mosses . . . . entire plants
Rock Tripes . . . . entire plants

Chapter 6

Freshwater Shores

FRESHWATER SHORES (LAKE, POND, OR STREAM EDGES) MAY be found in all of the other major inland habitats: forests, grasslands, deserts, and tundras. Swamps, bogs, and marshes are related shore-type habitats.

JERUSALEM ARTICHOKE *(Helianthus tuberosus)*

① This blossom is about 4 inches (101 mm) across. ② One of the two tubers is several inches from the stem *(left)*, and the width of largest leaf is about 2¹⁄₂ inches (64 mm).

KEY FEATURES A sunflower (both the central and the outer parts of the flower are yellow) with rough leaves and stems. Leaves are wide; the side veins are nearly parallel to the sawtooth leaf margins. Underground tubers. Up to 10 feet (3 m) tall.

SEASON AND USE *Summer–Spring:* Dig a few inches for the elongate **tubers** at the ends of runners, slightly away from the base of the plant. Raw or cooked (roasted, boiled). Raw tubers may taste like an unsweetened carrot; cooked tubers may taste like an earthy potato.

WHERE FOUND Freshwater shores, fields, roadsides, waste places, thickets, and fencerows. Eastern conterminous U.S. and south-central and southeastern Canada.

FRESHWATER / JERUSALEM ARTICHOKE

MINT (= FIELD MINT) (*Mentha arvensis*)

The middle flower cluster is ⁵/₈ inch (16 mm) across.

KEY FEATURES Leaves are paired (opposite) and have sawtooth edges. Stems are square where cut across. Flowers appear where leaves join the stem and are reddish blue, pale purple, or white. Leaves emit a mint odor when bruised. Up to 2 feet (0.6 m) tall, often less.

SEASON AND USE *SUMMER–FALL:* When the plant is flowering, steep the **leaves** in hot water for an aromatic tea. Leaves can also flavor foods.

OTHER USES Bruise the **leaves** for a mint-odor pick-me-up. Also try a leaf tea for upset stomach. Sometimes rubbing leaves on the skin will repel mosquitoes.

WHERE FOUND Freshwater shores, damp soils. Much of U.S., including Alaska, and much of temperate Canada.

FRESHWATER / MINT

SILVERWEED (*Argentina anserina* = *Potentilla anserina*)

Blossom is 1 inch (25 mm) across.

KEY FEATURES Leaves are comprised of many paired, sawtooth leaflets that are silvery underneath. Flowers, which are on separate stalks from the leaves, are yellow and have five petals. The plant is low growing and spreads by runners. Long, fleshy roots are sent down at the joints on the runners. Flower stalks are up to 11 inches (279 mm) tall.

SEASON AND USE *FALL–SPRING:* Slender **roots,** raw or cooked (boiled or roasted). May taste like parsnips, sweet potatoes, or chestnuts.

WHERE FOUND Freshwater shores, low meadows, salty or alkaline soils, and seashores. Much of U.S., including Alaska, and much of temperate Canada.

WATERCRESS
(Nasturtium officinale = Rorippa nasturtium-aquaticum)

Blossoms are $3/16$ inch (5 mm) across.

KEY FEATURES Plants grow in dense, low-lying or floating clumps or mats. Leaves have three to nine egg-shaped, smooth-edged leaflets, the largest appearing at the tip of the group. Roots are white and threadlike. Flowers are four-petaled, tiny, white, and appear in small clusters. Up to 10 inches (254 mm) tall.

SEASON AND USE *ALL YEAR:* Pinch off **young stems** and **leaves**. Remove any insect larvae or snails. Eat raw in salad or cook (steam) like spinach as a potherb; may also add raw (chopped) or cooked watercress to soup. Dry and grind leaves for a seasoning. Their peppery taste may resemble that of radish or horseradish. High in vitamins A, C, and E. **CAUTION**: Avoid watercress suspected to have grown in polluted water.

WHERE FOUND Springs and edges of slow, clear streams. All states of conterminous U.S., including Alaska, and southern Canada.

Complete stems are
about 5$\frac{1}{2}$ feet
(1.7 m) in height.

KEY FEATURES Stem is smooth, circular or triangular (where cut across), pithy, with no leaves. A cluster of brown flower or seed spikes is at top of the stem. Up to 9 feet (2.7 m) tall.

SEASON AND USE *SPRING:* Young **shoots** and tender cores at the bases of older shoots, both raw and cooked (boiled or roasted). First peel away the spongy parts as for cattails (next).

FALL–SPRING: **Rootstocks** and **rootstock sprouts** at the tips of the rootstocks, cooked (boiled or roasted). Mash and swish starchy rootstocks in water for a flour to thicken soup. **CAUTION:** Avoid eating any part of the plant if it is suspected that it grew in polluted water.

WHERE FOUND Freshwater shores, marshes. Much of U.S., including Alaska, and much of temperate Canada.

FRESHWATER / BULRUSHES

CATTAILS (*Typhus* species)

① This flower head is $6^7/_8$ inches (175 mm) high. ② The curved, white, peeled shoot is $3^1/_4$ by $^1/_2$ inch (82 by 13 mm); also visible are two sprouts and part of the rootstock. ③ A bloom spike with papery husk (*far left*) and another (*far right*) at a later stage with pollen; the height of complete spike at right is $9^1/_2$ inches (241 mm).

KEY FEATURES Leaves are swordlike, upright, and have no midrib. Flower heads are sausagelike and appear on top of stiff, unbranched stems. Up to 9 feet (2.7 m) tall. **CAUTION:** Similar to the swordlike leaves of poisonous wild iris.

SEASON AND USE *SPRING–FALL:* **Young shoots**, $2^1/2$ feet (0.8 m) tall and less, which are harder to find in summer and fall. May also find

(continued next page)

edible shoots below the water's surface. Pull the shoots from the rootstocks; peel the spongy parts from the lower parts of the shoots to reach a firm, tender white core, which is easily cut with a knife. Raw or cooked (boiled); may taste like cucumber when eaten raw.

LATE SPRING–EARLY SUMMER: Gather the green **bloom spikes** while they are in papery husks. Boil and nibble buds from the stalk like corn on the cob. May also scrape the buds from the central stalks and add them to stews or soups. Later, golden **pollen** appears in place of the husked upper parts of the bloom spikes. Bend a spike into a container and shake it to release the pollen; add the pollen to wheat flour or use to thicken soup.

LATE SUMMER–SPRING: Hornlike **sprouts** at the tips of rootstocks, raw or cooked (boiled). **Rootstocks**, cooked (roasted); remove the outer covering, chew the starchy core, and spit out the fibers. Mash the rootstocks, swish them in water for a flour, and add the flour to thicken soup. **CAUTION:** Avoid eating any part of a plant that was submerged if it is suspected that the water is polluted; green bloom spikes and pollen above the water may be safe. Similar to poisonous, bitter-tasting wild iris rootstocks.

OTHER USES Stuff cattail **down** into boots or trousers for insulation in cold weather; use the dry down as tinder for starting campfires. Use the dried leaves and stems for a mattress or as wall insulation in shelters. Weave the leaves into mats. Where water is not obvious, cattails are good indicators of groundwater near the surface. Chew juicy young shoots for water.

WHERE FOUND Freshwater shores, marshes. Much of U.S., including Alaska, and southern and western Canada.

REED GRASS (= REED) *(Phragmites australis = P. co...*

The seed head at lower left is opened. The largest leaf here is 1³/₈ inches (35 mm) wide.

KEY FEATURES Purplish to gray plumelike flower clusters appear at the tops of the stems and change to fluffy, silky seed heads. Stems are jointed, hollow or with pith. Leaves are long, up to 2 inches (50 mm) wide. Plant is up to 13 feet (4 m) tall.

SEASON AND USE *SPRING–SUMMER:* **Young shoots**, cooked (boiled). Before they blossom, dry the **young plants**, pound them into a sweet flour and separate the fibers, mix the flour with water, and form into balls; roast or bake.

    SUMMER–SPRING: **Rootstocks** (pulled up with difficulty), cooked (boiled or roasted). Mash the rootstocks, swish them in water for a flour, and add to soup in order to thicken. **CAUTION:** Avoid eating any part of a plant that was submerged if it suspected that the water is polluted. Young stems above the water may be safe.

OTHER USES Where water is not obvious, reed grass is an indicator of groundwater near the surface. Stuff the fluffy seed heads into boots and trousers for insulation in cold weather. Use the dry stems for a mattress or as wall insulation in shelters. Use short lengths of the hollow stems as spouts for tapping maple sap or as straws for sipping water from seeps.

WHERE FOUND Freshwater shores, marshes, ditches. Much of conterminous U.S. and much of temperate Canada.

Plant or Plant Group	Parts Eaten

SPRING

FORBS

Jerusalem Artichoke	tubers
Silverweed	roots
Watercress	young stems and leaves

GRASSLIKE PLANTS

Bulrushes	shoots, rootstocks
Cattails	shoots, bloom spikes, sprouts, rootstocks
Reed Grass	shoots, young stems, rootstocks

SUMMER

FORBS

Jerusalem Artichoke	tubers
Mint	leaves (tea)
Watercress	young stems and leaves

GRASSLIKE PLANTS

Bulrushes	shoots, rootstocks
Cattails	shoots, bloom spikes, pollen, sprouts, rootstocks
Reed Grass	shoots, young stems, rootstocks

FALL

FORBS

Jerusalem Artichoke	tubers
Mint	leaves (tea)
Silverweed	roots
Watercress	young stems and leaves

GRASSLIKE PLANTS

Bulrushes	rootstocks, sprouts
Cattails	shoots, sprouts, rootstocks
Reed Grass	rootstocks

WINTER

FORBS

Jerusalem Artichoke	tubers
Silverweed	roots
Watercress	young stems and leaves

GRASSLIKE PLANTS

Bulrushes	rootstocks, sprouts
Cattails	rootstocks, sprouts
Reed Grass	rootstocks

Chapter 7

Seacoasts

SOME PLANTS THAT CHARACTERISTICALLY INHABIT SEACOASTS also live inland. Among such wide-ranging plants are beach pea, orache, and glasswort, all of which are described in this chapter.

The taste and texture of seaweeds, plantlike algae that live in the sea, may require you to test these plants with an open mind. It may take time to get used to them. Four of the more common and better-tasting groups are included here.

BEACH PEA *(Lathyrus japonicus = L. maritimus)*

Pods are 2 inches (50 mm) long.

KEY FEATURES Plants are upright or sprawling. Flowers are pealike and purple to violet. Leaves are of many leaflets, are ellipse shaped to egg shaped, and have smooth edges. Stems end in curling **tendrils** ("threads"). Seedpods form after the blossoms and resemble those of garden peas but are smaller. Up to about 2 feet (0.6 m) tall.

SEASON AND USE *SUMMER:* **Young**, tender **pods**, raw or cooked (boiled or steamed), like snow peas. Later, shell the bright green, tender **seeds**, eat raw or cooked (boiled or steamed). Add the pods and seeds to soups. Rich in vitamin A and protein. **CAUTION:** Some wild peas are poisonous; be careful with identification, and try questionable plants only in small amounts. Consult a botanical manual for precise identification.

WHERE FOUND Sandy or gravelly shores. New Jersey to Hudson Bay and Greenland, California to Alaska. Also Great Lakes area.

ORACHES (*Atriplex patula* and similar species)

The largest leaf blade here is 3⅝ inches (92 mm) long.

KEY FEATURES Related to lamb's-quarters (see page 32) and four-wing saltbush (see page 45). Leaves are triangular, arrowhead shaped or lance shaped, with irregular sawtooth edges; salty; and often have a mealy covering, especially on the undersides. Flowers are tiny and appear in greenish clusters. Up to 5 feet (1.5 m) tall but often less. Often found with glassworts (see the following).

SEASON AND USE *SPRING–FALL:* Pinch off the **young**, tender, upper **leaves**. Eat raw in salads or steam or boil them until they are easily cut with a spoon or a flat stick. One of the best potherbs; resembles spinach. Rich in iron.

WHERE FOUND Along seacoasts, just above high-tide line, especially along the edges of salt marshes. Inland, on salty and alkaline soils, also in salt marshes. Florida to Labrador, California to Alaska, and much of inland U.S. and Canada.

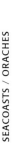

GLASSWORTS (*Salicornia* species)

These stems are up to $3/16$ inch (5 mm) across.

KEY FEATURES Upright or sprawling, with small green spikes. Plants seem to lack leaves and flowers. Stems are juicy, salty, and jointed; have opposite branches; and are light green in spring and summer, and tend to turn yellowish to reddish in the fall. Up to 16 inches (406 mm) tall. Often found with oraches (see the preceding).

SEASON AND USE *SPRING–FALL:* Tender **stem tops** and the **tips of side branches**, raw or cooked (better, boiled). Avoid the older parts of the plant, which have a central, tough, inedible fiber.

WHERE FOUND Along seacoasts, near high-tide line, especially along edges of salt marshes; may be submerged at high tide. Inland, on salty and alkaline soils, also in salt marshes. Coastal Texas to Newfoundland, Baja California to Alaska, and much of inland U.S. and Canada.

ROCKWEEDS (*Pelvetiopsis* species and *Fucus* species)

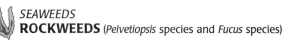

The branches above the swollen tips are up to 1³/₈ inches (35 mm) wide.

KEY FEATURES Of many flattened, equal branches, with mature branches swollen at the tips. Branches have midribs (*Fucus*) or not (*Pelvetiopsis*). Olive green to brownish or yellowish when wet, darker when dry. Up to 20 inches (508 mm) long.

SEASON AND USE *ALL YEAR (BEST DURING SPRING–SUMMER):* Rockweeds without midribs may be better tasting than those with midribs. First remove any snails, which is easily done by dipping the rockweed in fresh water. Harvest the tender **tips of branches**. Eat raw or, better, cook (boil) in soup. Can dry for later use, which includes use as a salty seasoning. *Fucus* is high in protein and vitamin A.

WHERE FOUND Upper to middle intertidal zone on rocky shores; may be washed ashore. California to Alaska, North Carolina to Maritime Provinces.

SEACOASTS / ROCKWEEDS

 **SEA LETTUCES** (*Ulva* species)

This mass, measuring 5$^7/_8$ inches (149 mm high), clings to boulders and pebbles.

KEY FEATURES Frond is thin, filmy, bright green, translucent, and often has ruffled edges. Up to 2 feet (0.6 m) long.

SEASON AND USE *ALL YEAR (BEST DURING SPRING–SUMMER):* **Fronds,** raw (chopped fine in salads), cooked (boiled) as a potherb, or added to soups. Remove any sand and discard torn edges. Also can be dried and powdered as a salty seasoning for other foods; fronds dry quickly. High in protein, calcium, iron, and vitamin A.

WHERE FOUND Upper to middle intertidal zone of rocky shores and mudflats; may be washed ashore. Atlantic and Pacific Coasts of U.S., including Alaska, and Canada.

SEA PALM (*Postelsia palmaeformis*)

Averaging about 12 inches (310 mm) tall, this sea palm holds fast to rocky, wave-bashed shore.

KEY FEATURES Resembles miniature olive to brown palm tree; often grows in clumps. Blades in crown at top of hollow stalk are anchored to rocks by a holdfast, are straplike, and are grooved lengthwise. Up to 2 feet (0.6 m) tall.

SEASON AND USE *ALL YEAR (BEST DURING SPRING–SUMMER):* **Blades** and **stalks**, raw, steamed, or added to soups. Blades may be dried in the sun. **CAUTION:** Gather sparingly so plants may readily reproduce themselves. Can gather plants cast upon the shore.

WHERE FOUND British Columbia to central California. Attached to wave-bashed rocks in the middle intertidal zone. Often found with mussels and stalked barnacles.

SEACOASTS / SEA PALM

WINGED KELPS (*Alaria* species)

The widest part of the foreground frond is 6⁷/₈ inches (175 mm).

KEY FEATURES Large, olive-green to brown, wavy-edged fronds or blades with a flattened midrib. At the base of the main frond is a short stem and holdfast for attachment to rocks. Between the main frond and the holdfast are smaller, tonguelike side fronds. Main frond is up to 10 feet (3 m) long.

SEASON AND USE *All Year (Best During Spring–Summer):* Thinly sliced **midrib**, raw or added to soups. Tonguelike **side fronds,** fresh or dried (better) as a cooked (boiled) vegetable, a salty seasoning, or added to soups. Remove any shells and discard torn edges. Harvest the side fronds conservatively since they are necessary for reproduction. Rich in vitamin C, calcium, and protein.

WHERE FOUND Lower intertidal zone of rocky shores; may be washed ashore. Cape Cod to the Arctic, California to Alaska.

SEACOAST PLANTS BY SEASON

Plant or Plant Group   **Parts Eaten**

SPRING

FORBS
Oraches . . . . young leaves

GRASSLIKE PLANTS
Glassworts . . . . stem and branch tips

SEAWEEDS
Rockweeds . . . . branch tips
Sea Lettuces . . . . fronds
Sea Palm . . . . blades and stalks
Winged Kelps . . . . midribs, side fronds

SUMMER

FORBS
Beach Pea . . . . young pods, seeds
Oraches . . . . young leaves

GRASSLIKE PLANTS
Glassworts . . . . stem and branch tips

SEAWEEDS
Rockweeds . . . . branch tips
Sea Lettuces . . . . fronds
Sea Palm . . . . blades and stalks
Winged Kelps . . . . midribs, side fronds

FALL

FORBS
Oraches . . . . young leaves

GRASSLIKE PLANTS
Glassworts . . . . stem and branch tips

SEAWEEDS
Rockweeds . . . . branch tips
Sea Lettuces . . . . fronds
Sea Palm . . . . blades and stalks
Winged Kelps . . . . midribs, side fronds

WINTER

SEAWEEDS
Rockweeds . . . . branch tips
Sea Lettuces . . . . fronds
Sea Palm . . . . blades and stalks
Winged Kelps . . . . midribs, side fronds

Chapter 8

Other Useful Plants

MANY PLANTS ARE NOT EDIBLE BUT HAVE OTHER USES. THIS chapter provides a selection of such plants, which are distributed widely.

SNOWBRUSHES (= SOAPBLOOMS) (*Ceanothus* species)

The leaf at far right is 1¹/₂ inches (38 mm) long.

KEY FEATURES Evergreen or deciduous shrubs. Leaves are often egg shaped and finely sawtooth but may be narrow with smooth edges; main veins tend to parallel the leaf edges. Tiny flowers are in dense clusters and are white or lilac. Up to 13 feet (4 m) tall but are often much less.

SEASON AND USE *SUMMER:* Rub the **flower clusters** between your hands or crush them in water to release a soap. Some kinds of snow-brushes are better as a soap source than others. (Some kinds, like New Jersey Tea, make a good tea from dried **leaves**.)

WHERE FOUND Woods, roadsides, rocky ground, and prairies. Much of conterminous U.S. and southern Canada.

OTHER USEFUL PLANTS / SNOWBRUSHES

76

WILLOWS (*Salix* species)

The leaf in the left-central foreground is 2⅝ inches (67 mm) long.

KEY FEATURES Mostly shrubs but also trees; may form dense thickets. Twigs are often colorful: yellow, orange, red, or olive green. Leaves are mostly long and narrow, are pointed at both ends, and are usually finely sawtooth. Leaf and flower buds hug the twigs and are covered by a single, caplike scale; neither leaf nor flower buds are at the very tips of twigs. Tiny flowers are in dense clusters called **catkins**, which are often fuzzy and caterpillar shaped; some bring to mind the "pussies" of "pussy willows."

SEASON AND USE *ALL YEAR:* Chew the **leaves** or **bark** for headache or pain; both contain salicin (*SAL-uh-suhn*), a substance related to the active ingredient in aspirin. The leaves and the bark can also be brewed as a pain-relieving tea. Try placing the chewed leaves on insect stings. **CAUTION**: Don't use if you are allergic to aspirin.

SPRING: **Young leaves** of some willows are good to eat raw. High in vitamin C. Expect bitterness from most willows.

WHERE FOUND Mostly along streams and other freshwater shores and in moist soils. Most of U.S., including Alaska, and Canada.

GRASSLANDS: FORBS
MULLEIN (*Verbascum thapsus*)

The tallest plant here is 79 inches (2 m) high.

KEY FEATURES Plant is covered with woolly hairs; has upright, single or branched stems. Leaves are large and lance shaped. Yellow flowers are in spikes that form during the second year; dead, brown spikes last well beyond the second year. Up to 8 feet (2.4 m) tall.

SEASON AND USE *SPRING–FALL:* Soft, velvety **leaves** as a substitute for toilet paper. May try tea from the **flowers** or from fresh or dried **leaves**, best picked while the plant is blossoming, for the relief of chest colds or coughing. Strain the tea through a cloth to remove the throat-irritating leaf hairs. Dip the flower stalks in evergreen pitch for use as torches. If short of socks, try leaves to line footwear.

WHERE FOUND Grasslands, roadsides, railroad grades, old fields, waste places, rocky banks, open woods, pastures, and fencerows. Most of conterminous U.S. and southern Canada.

 **YARROWS** (*Achillea* species)

The entire cluster of flowers is 4 inches (102 mm) across.

KEY FEATURES Flowers are small, arranged in flat-topped clusters, and are white, sometimes pink or yellow. Leaves are aromatic, narrow, and divided into fine filaments. Up to 3 feet (0.9 m) tall. **CAUTION**: Similar to poison hemlock (see page 94) and water hemlocks (see page 95).

SEASON AND USE *Spring–Summer:* To stop bleeding (and reduce pain), mash or bruise the **leaves** and place them on wounds. Can also be used to stop nosebleeds. May try a yarrow tea from the leaves as a disinfectant. May try rubbing the bruised or mashed **leaves** on the skin for use as an insect repellent. **CAUTION**: Some persons may experience a skin irritation as a reaction to yarrow.

WHERE FOUND Grasslands, roadsides, waste places, fields, open woods, thickets, and shores. Most of U.S., including Alaska, and much of temperate Canada.

OTHER USEFUL PLANTS / YARROWS

This blossom is 2¹/₄ inches (57 mm) across.

SEASON AND USE *SPRING–FALL:* Where water is not obvious, irises are indicators of groundwater near the surface.

Described in chapter 10, Common Poisonous Plants, page 96.

HORSETAILS (= SCOURING RUSHES) (*Equisetum* species)

① The sterile plant, 14 inches (356 mm) high, bears branches in whorls at the joints.
② The fertile plant bears a cone 1 1/8 inches (28 mm) high.

KEY FEATURES Hollow stems separate at the joints; stems have tiny ridges. Fertile stems bear cones at their tips; sterile stems bear branches in whorls at the joints and resemble green horsetails. Hard silica crystals are present in the stems. Up to 5 feet (1.5 m) tall but are usually 3 feet (0.9 m) and less.

SEASON AND USE *SPRING–FALL:* Abrasive **stems** can be used as scouring pads for scrubbing pots or polishing any hard surface. Use the larger fertile stems to sharpen knives. May also use the stems to scrub your face and hands. Because many scouring rushes live in wet places, they can indicate groundwater near the surface.

WHERE FOUND Freshwater shores, ditches, roadsides, seepage areas, meadows, fields, waste places, marshes, wet woodlands, embankments, and thickets. All of U.S., including Alaska, and all of Canada.

Chapter 9

Are Edible Wild Plants Nutritious?

THE SKEPTIC IN US MIGHT ASK, "DO EDIBLE WILD PLANTS HAVE ANY real nutritional value? Are they worth the trouble to identify, harvest, and prepare?"

Instead of an unqualified "yes" or "no," a better approach is to turn to food charts, lists of foods analyzed for various nutrients. These make for more meaningful comparisons.

But read the food charts with care, and don't take them too literally or consider them absolute. Realize that the values given are averages, and that they may vary widely with individual tests. Ask these questions: Where was the plant grown? When was the plant harvested? What were the growing conditions? How many plants were harvested?

84

Below I've compiled many nutrients for eight wild vegetables and for eight common domesticated vegetables.

NUTRITIONAL VALUES OF SELECTED WILD EDIBLE PLANTS PER 100 GRAMS OF FOOD

	Water g	Calories kCal	Protein g	Carbohydrate g	Calcium mg	Iron mg	Potassium mg	Vit. C mg	Vit. A IU
Burdock root (*Arctium lappa*, raw) 80.09	80.09	72	1.53	17.35	41	0.80	308	3	0
Dandelion greens (*Taraxacum officinale*, raw) 85.60	85.60	45	2.70	9.20	187	3.10	397	35	14,000
Dock root (*Rumex*, raw) .93.00	93.00	22	2.00	3.20	44	2.40	390	48	4,000
Jerusalem Artichoke root (*Helianthus annuus*, raw) . 78.01	78.01	76	2.00	17.44	14	3.40	429	4	20
Lamb's-quarters (*Chenopodium album*, raw). 84.30	84.30	43	4.20	7.30	309	1.20	452	80	11,600
Salsify root (*Tragopogon porrifolius*, raw) 77.00	77.00	82	3.30	18.60	60	0.70	380	8	0
Seaweed, laver (*Porphyra laciniata*, raw) 85.03	85.03	35	5.81	5.11	70	1.80	356	39	5,202
Watercress (*Nasturtium officinale*, raw) 95.11	95.11	11	2.30	1.29	120	0.20	330	43	4,700

Source: U.S. Department of Agriculture, Agriculture Research Service, Nutrient Data Laboratory, Nutrient Database for Standard Reference, Release 13, Dec. 1999 (www.nalusda.gov/fnic/index.html).

NUTRITIONAL VALUES OF SELECTED CULTIVATED EDIBLE PLANTS PER 100 GRAMS OF FOOD

	Water g	Calories kcal	Protein g	Carbohydrate g	Calcium mg	Iron mg	Potassium mg	Vit. C mg	Vit. A IU
Beans, lima (raw)	70.24	113	6.84	20.16	34	3.14	467	23.4	303
Cabbage (raw)	92.15	25	1.44	5.43	47	0.59	246	32.2	133
Celery (raw)	94.64	16	0.75	3.65	40	0.40	287	7.0	134
Lettuce, looseleaf (raw)	94.00	18	1.30	3.50	68	1.40	264	18.0	1,900
Peppers, sweet (raw)	92.19	27	0.89	6.43	9	0.46	177	89.3	632
Potato, flesh & skin (raw)	78.96	79	2.07	17.98	7	0.76	543	19.7	0
Spinach (raw)	91.58	22	2.86	3.50	99	2.71	558	28.1	6,715
Tomato, red (raw)	93.76	21	0.85	4.64	5	0.45	222	19.1	623

Source: U.S. Department of Agriculture, Agriculture Research Service, Nutrient Data Laboratory, Nutrient Database for Standard Reference, Release 13, Dec. 1999 (*www.nalusda.gov/fnic/index.html*).

NUTRITION

Lamb's-quarters and laver seaweed are similar to lima beans in protein content. Burdock, Jerusalem artichoke, and salsify are similar to lima beans and potato in carbohydrates. Dandelion and lamb's-quarters are higher in calcium than lettuce and spinach. Dandelion contains as much iron as lima beans. The wild vegetables are closely comparable with the domesticated vegetables in potassium content. (For further comparison, dandelion, dock, Jerusalem artichoke, and lamb's-quarters equal or exceed the potassium content of a raw banana, which is rich in potassium at 396 mg.)

Dock, lamb's-quarters, laver seaweed, and watercress are higher in vitamin C than the domesticated vegetables except for peppers. (Raw oranges, thought to be unusually high in vitamin C, have an average value of 53.2 mg, less than that found in either lamb's-quarters or peppers.) Dandelion, dock, lamb's-quarters, laver seaweed, and watercress surpass all the domesticated vegetables, except spinach, in vitamin A.

Let's now turn to a brief comparison with wild nuts. Raw acorns have a protein content of 6.15 grams and a fat content of 23.86 grams per 100 grams of an analyzed sample. But piñon nuts rank at a whopping 11.57 grams of protein and 60.98 grams of fat! In beef hot dogs, these values compare at 12.00 grams of protein and 28.50 grams of fat.

To conclude: you can acquire sufficient nutrients from edible wild plants to maintain your health. And these plants are as nutritious or more nutritious than domesticated plants. But should this be surprising? Remember, all domesticated plants are derived from wild stock.

Chapter 10

Common Poisonous Plants

HUNDREDS OF PLANTS IN THE U.S. AND CANADA ARE KNOWN to be poisonous. Included here are nine plants or plant groups that you are most likely to encounter.

CAUTION: If you suspect that you have eaten a poisonous plant, call the nearest Poison Control Center immediately for aid. You can also call 911 for a medical emergency.

POISON IVY (*Toxicodendron radicans*) and
POISON OAKS (*T. diversilobum* and *T. quercifolium*)

① The largest poison ivy leaflet here is 4 inches (101 mm) long; ② poison ivy berries are $3/16$ inch (5 mm) across.

KEY FEATURES Poison ivy is a shrub or vine. Leaves are most often of three leaflets ("leaves of three, let it be") that tend to droop; leaflets are egg shaped, their edges sawtooth or smooth, and turn red or gold in the fall. Flowers are small, whitish or cream-colored, in clusters that arise from where leafstalks join the stem. Berries are white or yellowish-white. Poison ivy is most often low-growing but can reach 9 feet (2.7 m) tall. Poison oaks tend to have leaflets lobed like oak leaves and may be hairy.

POISONOUS PARTS All; oil from brushing against the plants causes a severe skin irritation in most people.

SYMPTOMS Itching and skin rash, formation of oozing blisters. Eating leaves or berries may cause serious stomach and intestinal disorders (birds, though, eat the berries without apparent harm). If you suspect contact, wash the affected areas immediately. ·

WHERE FOUND Forests, thickets, ravines, freshwater shores, fencerows, waste places. Most of conterminous U.S. and southern Canada.

POISONOUS / POISON IVY AND POISON OAKS

FORESTS: FORBS
BANEBERRIES *(Actaea* species)

These berries
are $^3/_8$ inch
(10 mm) across.

KEY FEATURES Leaves are divided into several leaflets with sharp, sawtooth edges. Berries are white (tipped with a dark spot) or red, in a cluster at the top of the upright stem. Flowers are small and whitish, in rounded clusters. Up to 3 feet (0.9 m) tall.

POISONOUS PARTS All, but especially the berries and roots.

SYMPTOMS Severe irritation of the stomach and intestines, dizziness, vomiting, diarrhea, headache, paralysis, cardiac arrest.

WHERE FOUND Forests, thickets, streambanks, bogs, and near springs. Most of U.S., including Alaska, and much of temperate Canada.

POISONOUS / BANEBERRIES

**DATURAS (*duh-TOUR-uhz*) (= SACRED DATURAS = JI
SONWEEDS = JAMESTOWN WEEDS)** (*Datura* species)

The largest flower here is about 3 inches (76 mm) across.

KEY FEATURES Bad-smelling weeds. Flowers are large and trumpet shaped and are white, purple, or rose. Leaves are large, alternate on the stem, and are egg shaped with coarse, sawtooth edges. Seedpods are rounded, prickly. Up to 5 feet (1.5 m) tall.

POISONOUS PARTS All, but especially the seeds, leaves, and roots.

SYMPTOMS Intense thirst, disturbed vision (may last up to two weeks), flushed skin, delirium, rapid and weak heartbeat, convulsions, coma, possible violent behavior.

WHERE FOUND Grasslands, barnyards, pastures, waste places, cropland, feedlots. Most of conterminous U.S. and southern Canada.

POISONOUS / DATURAS

NIGHTSHADES (*Solanum carolinense, S. dulcamara, S. nigrum = S. americanum*, and others)

① The leaf at top with flowers and buds is 1¹³/₁₆ inches (46 mm) long; ② the largest nightshade fruit is ⁵/₁₆ inch (8 mm) long.

KEY FEATURES Bushy weeds in the same family as the potato and tomato. Leaves are egg shaped, lance shaped, or triangular, alternate on the stem; edges are sawtooth, smooth, or lobed. Stems are smooth, hairy, or prickly. Flowers are five-petaled, in clusters, and are violet, purple, blue, white, or yellow; center of the flower is often formed into a yellow, conelike beak. Berries resemble miniature tomatoes and are black, red, orange, or yellow. Up to 3 feet (0.9 m) tall or 8 feet (2.4 m) long if vinelike.

POISONOUS PARTS All, but especially the unripe berries. Poisonous qualities vary with the person, species, and place of growth. Some people can eat the berries without suffering ill effects, but it is best to avoid them.

SYMPTOMS Stomach and intestinal irritation, nausea, vomiting, diarrhea or constipation, loss of appetite, paralysis.

WHERE FOUND Grasslands, waste places, cultivated fields, thickets, open woods, roadsides, seashores, freshwater shores, pastures, ditches, fencerows. Most of U.S., including Alaska, and southern Canada.

DEATH CAMASES (*CAM-uh-suhz*)
(*Zigadenus* species = *Zygadenus* species)

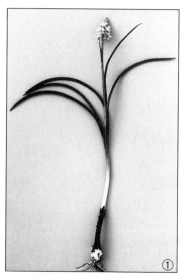

① The height of this plant, from the base of the bulb to the top of the flower cluster, is 14.5 inches (368 mm); bulb, $3/4$ inch (19 mm) across, is $4^{1}/_{2}$ inches (114 mm) below ground level. ② The flower cluster is 2 inches (50 mm) high.

KEY FEATURES Leaves are grasslike, arise from near the base of the plant, and are V-shaped where cut across. Flowers are in a long cluster and are greenish-white, yellow, or pink. Bulb is onionlike but without the onion odor. Up to 5 feet (1.5 m) tall but often much less. **CAUTION:** Similar in appearance to nonpoisonous camas, wild onion, and sego lily.

POISONOUS PARTS All, but especially the bulb—even when dried.

SYMPTOMS Gastrointestinal irritation, frothing at the mouth, lowering of body temperature, coma, nausea.

WHERE FOUND Grasslands, pinelands, shores, bogs. Most of U.S., including Alaska, and much of temperate Canada.

POISONOUS / DEATH CAMASES

FALSE HELLEBORES (*HELL-uh-borz*) (= CORN LILIES)
(*Veratrum* species)

This undeveloped
flower stalk (*top*) is
4 inches (102 mm) long.

KEY FEATURES Leaves are up to 12 inches (305 mm) long, egg shaped or elliptical, with pleats and parallel veins; they clasp the stem in three rows. Flowers are in a branched cluster up to 2 feet (0.6 m) tall and are white, greenish-white, or yellowish-green. Seeds have broad wings. Rootstock is thick, fibrous. Up to 8 feet (2.4 m) tall.

POISONOUS PARTS All, especially the rootstocks and young shoots.

SYMPTOMS Frothing at the mouth, shortness of breath, slowing of heartbeat, burning of the mouth and throat, hallucination, headache, blurred vision, vomiting, diarrhea, lockjaw, stomach cramps, cardiac arrest.

WHERE FOUND Freshwater shores, wet meadows, swamps, moist woods, pastures. Most of U.S., including Alaska, and much of temperate Canada.

POISONOUS / FALSE HELLEBORES

93

POISON HEMLOCK (*Conium maculatum*)

① These flower clusters are 1³/₄ inches (44 mm) across. ② The leaf segment, of several leaflets, is 3¹/₄ inches (82 mm) long.

KEY FEATURES Similar to water hemlock (see next). Has a musty odor when bruised. Hollow stem often has purple spots. Flowers are in umbrella-like clusters and are white. Leaves are fernlike, of several leaflets, with sawtooth edges; main veins end at tips of leaf points rather than at notches. Fleshy roots usually are single. Lowest stem and rootstock have few or no chambers and cross partitions when cut lengthwise, not often well-displayed as in water hemlocks. Up to 10 feet (3 m) tall. **CAUTION**: Similar in appearance to nonpoisonous wild carrot, wild parsley, and wild parsnip, and to seeds of anise or dill. Wash your hands after handling this plant.

POISONOUS PARTS All, but especially the seeds.

SYMPTOMS Nausea, convulsions, vomiting, paralysis, coma, slowing of the heart, weakening of muscles. Eating the plant may not always be fatal. Used to put Socrates to death.

WHERE FOUND Freshwater shores, waste places, ditches, roadsides, fencerows, edges of cultivated fields. Most of conterminous U.S. and southern Canada.

POISONOUS / POISON HEMLOCK

WATER HEMLOCKS (*Circuta* species)

① The larger flower clusters here are 2³/₄ inches (70 mm) across. ② The leaflet in the lower right corner is 2¹/₂ inches (64 mm) long. ③ The width of the hollow stem (sliced through) is ³/₄ inch (19 mm), and below it is the cluster of rootstocks.

KEY FEATURES Similar to poison hemlock. Stem is hollow. Flowers are in umbrella-like clusters and are white or greenish. Leaves are comprised of several narrow leaflets with sawtooth edges; main veins tend to end at the notches of leaf edges rather than at the points. Fleshy roots are usually several to a cluster and resemble parsnips. When cut lengthwise, the lowest stem and rootstock often show chambers separated by cross partitions; cut surface oozes a yellowish oily fluid with the pungent odor of parsnip. Up to 7 feet (2.1 m) tall . **CAUTION**: Similar in appearance to nonpoisonous wild parsnip and water parsnip.

POISONOUS PARTS All. Most poisonous plant group in the North Temperate Zone.

SYMPTOMS Frothing at the mouth, tremors, spasmodic convulsions, abdominal pain, dilation of the pupils, high temperature, delirium, nausea, death. Six men rafting on the Owyhee River (Oregon) in 1984 ate water hemlock roots, apparently thinking they were parsnips. After about 45 minutes the guide had a seizure and later died, another man also had a seizure but survived, and the remainder had to be treated for poisoning. The severity of the effects varied with the amount consumed. One survivor said the roots tasted like a carrot but were a little bitter.

WHERE FOUND Freshwater shores, marshes, swamps, ditches, wet meadows, pastures. Most of U.S., including Alaska, and much of temperate Canada.

IRISES (= BLUE FLAGS) (*Iris* species)

This blossom is
2¹/₄ inches
(57 mm) across.

KEY FEATURES Similar to garden iris. Leaves are swordlike. Flowers are large, of nine conspicuous parts in three groups that radiate from the center, and are blue, violet, purple, yellow, or white. Rootstocks are horizontal, with a disagreeable bitter taste. Up to 3 feet (0.9 m) tall.
CAUTION: Similar in appearance to nonpoisonous cattails.

POISONOUS PARTS All, but especially the rootstocks.

SYMPTOMS Irritation of the stomach and intestines. May cause the mouth and throat to burn. Handling the plants may cause a skin rash in some persons.

WHERE FOUND Freshwater shores, wet meadows, marshes, seashores, swamps, ditches, bogs, woods. Most of U.S., including Alaska, and much of temperate Canada.

Chapter 11

Finding Water

YOU MAY SURVIVE MANY DAYS OR EVEN A FEW WEEKS WITH LITTLE or no food, but only a few days without water.

Water makes up one-half to three-fourths of human adult bodies—about 10 to 12 gallons, depending on body fat. A closer look shows water constitutes nearly 85% of the brain, about 80% of the blood, about 70% of lean muscle, 25% of fat, and 22% of bone. That we are creatures of water is further evident by our floating in the "amniotic sea" for nine months. If we don't continually replenish this essential fluid, we succumb to dehydration.

DEHYDRATION SIGNS AND EFFECTS

Clear signs of dehydration include obvious thirst; dry mouth; dry, pale, and wrinkled skin without its normal elasticity; sunken eyes; and decreased urination that is dark. A sure sign of dehydration is dark urine, when it is brownish rather than the normal yellow. Dehydration is aggravated by excessive sweating, hemorrhaging, diarrhea, and vomiting.

If left unresolved, what can dehydration do to you? Among the effects are weakness, confusion and mental instability, lightheadedness or fainting, reduced blood pressure, a faster heart and breathing rate, muscle spasms and cramps, nausea, poor judgment, and lessened vision. The ultimate effect, of course, is collapse and death, which occurs when 15 to 25% of the body's water is lost.

Most of us never experience the severe effects of dehydration. With prolonged, extreme exertion in hot weather, though, they may become immediate and real.

How much water do we need to avoid dehydration? The much-touted eight glasses per day is an average. Some people get by on considerably less. Pat Quesnel, the first to travel from the U.S. Pacific Coast to the Hawaiian Islands in a dory in 1976, discovered a gallon of water would last him about three days. And his trip was not short—111 days. Specific amounts of needed water depend on our body weight, air temperature, and exertion. Remember, too, that dehydration can occur during cold conditions as well as hot.

CONSERVING WATER

When short of water, the natural tendency is to drink less. A better approach, though, is not to ration water, but drink when you feel the urge. Carry the water in your stomach rather than in your water bottle or canteen. And fill up what your stomach will hold at each water source.

If you shouldn't ration water, how else might you conserve it? In dry, hot places, seek shade, and don't travel during the hottest times of the day. When you need to move, do so slowly. To cut down on water loss through sweating, wear loose-fitting, preferably light-colored clothing and a hat. Breathe through your nose rather than your mouth to cut back on water loss through exhalation. (Through sweating and breathing, along with urinating and bowel movements, you can lose much or most of your daily quota of water.) And if you have little or no water, hold off on eating, which requires considerable water consumption unless the foods are particularly juicy.

FINDING WATER

Plant Indicators

To locate water, a good first approach is to take notice of water-loving plants. Some plants just can't survive far from water. Among the water-loving trees are cottonwoods, which usually have broad and coarsely sawtooth leaves and cottony seeds; and sycamores, which have bark that peels in irregular patches, maplelike leaves, and flowers in globelike heads. Both trees appear often along streams.

Common water-loving shrubs include willows (see page 77) and saltcedars (or tamarisks). The Eurasian-derived saltcedars, also of tree size, sport reddish-brown or purple twigs, scalelike leaves, and pink or white flowers in fingerlike clusters. Expect both willows and saltcedars along freshwater shores or growing on other moist soils.

Among the good, nonwoody, water-indicating plants are cattails (see page 61), reed grass (see page 63), irises (see page 96), and most horsetails (see page 81). These plants are especially useful where water is not obvious but groundwater is near the surface.

Animal Indicators

Be aware of a few animal indicators of nearby water. Larger plant-eating mammals require a steady source of water. Following their game trails downhill will often lead you to a water source.

Birds may be useful indicators. Smaller seed-eating birds generally stick close to water. Watch for their flocks or listen for their twittering. Cliff swallows require mud to build their distinctive juglike or gourdlike nests. Keep your eye on the sky for large, easy-to-spot wading birds such as the great blue heron, or such aquatic birds as ducks, geese, pelicans, and cormorants. Watch their movements; all these birds depend on water as a source for their food.

Geology and Water

A little knowledge of geology will aid you in your water quest. Part of the precipitation that strikes the ground follows two paths: it washes or flows over the surface to find its way into streams, lakes, or ponds or it soaks into the ground. (Much rain and snow evaporates or indirectly **transpires** through the leaves of plants.) When water at the surface is inaccessible, you must turn to the **groundwater** that has soaked into the ground.

Water seeps into the ground because of spaces or voids. In loose sediment or loose rock the spaces are tiny and appear between mineral or rock particles that make up the sediment or rock. In "hard" or "tight" rocks the spaces are often larger and result from cracks or fractures, cavities dissolved in such rocks as limestone, and holes in lava flows from trapped gas bubbles. For water to move readily through sediment or rock, though, the spaces must be interconnected. Sand, sandstone, gravel, and **conglomerate** (lithified gravel) tend to allow water to move through them because of interconnected spaces, whereas mud (clay and silt) and **shale** (lithified mud) do not, unless the shale is cracked or fractured.

As snail-paced groundwater trickles through interconnected openings, it eventually saturates the ground at some depth. The top of the saturated zone is called the **water table**. The water table tends to imitate the lay of the land's surface: flat where the country is flat, higher at the hills and lower in the valleys. Springs, marshes, ponds, swamps, lakes, and permanent streams are places where the water table meets the ground surface. In dry regions, most streams are actually above the water table and tend to lose their water through soaking into the ground.

In places, a "tight" clay or shale without interconnected openings may trap or collect water from porous rocks above the main water table to form a local **perched water table**. Here you can find springs on a hillside or cliff well above where you would normally expect them. Lush vegetation, including cattails and reed grass, helps you spot such places from a distance.

Once you are familiar with the behavior of groundwater, you can keep an eye out for several possible sources of water. Seek out the generally purer water of springs along the edges of streams. Look in the caverns and cavities of limestones for springs. Search lava rocks. If no seeps exude from trapped gas-bubble holes in lava flows, look for long vertical cracks that separate lava rocks into columns. Water may ooze from the base of the columns. In other hard rocks like granite, water may issue from irregular, crisscrossing cracks.

Scan sea cliffs along seacoasts for springs discharging from perched water tables. On ocean beaches, look for rivulets flowing seaward when the tide is out. In coastal sand dunes, and inland dunes as well, seek out possible surface water in the deeper depressions, especially during spring and early summer. Clay and silt or shale beneath the sand may cause the water table to be near the surface.

Digging for water is sensible in only a few situations. You might dig in the lowest depressions of sand dunes. If the sand is moist, dig and wait for any water to seep into the hole. Line the hole with sticks to prevent the hole from caving in. In coastal dunes, only the shallowest water is apt to be fresh because it floats on the more dense salty water that may have seeped in under the dunes. Some springs require digging to increase the flow or to create a basin in which meager water can collect. Suck the water directly or sip with a straw fashioned from the hollow stem of reed grass (see page 63). You might also try to dig in a dry streambed, but only at the outside of a bend in the deepest part of the streambed. Pursue this source only if the stream sediment is moist.

Collecting Dew and Rainwater

Collecting dew is one of the easiest and safest ways to acquire water. If desperate, lick the dew off plants and objects, but avoid the dew from plants such as those covered in chapter 10. With a bandanna or other cloth, mop the dew and wring

it into your mouth or a container. You might also try a h̶
of grass to sop up the dew. Another approach is to tie
grass tufts to your ankles and walk through dew-laden plants.
As when foraging plants for food, don't collect dew along
roadsides, fields, and other places where pesticides may have
been sprayed.

Lick and mop rain-laden leaves of trees, shrubs, and forbs as
you would collect dew. To catch rainwater, lay plastic sheets or
rainwear in ground depressions. Dam up small, dry streambeds
to create catch basins. Search for rainwater trapped in tree-trunk
cavities or in potholes dissolved on fairly flat rock surfaces.

Water from Plants

Plants in themselves may be sources of water. In early spring,
during frosty nights followed by warm days, tap maples (see
page 9), birches, and other trees for their watery sap. In dry
regions, turn to cacti (see page 47). Remove spines, chew the
fleshy parts, and suck out the water. Or mash, squeeze, and
strain out the water.

An almost effortless yet reliable method to extract water
from plants is by means of a **solar tree still**, providing you had
the forethought to bring clear plastic bags. I'd recommend
bags at least 2 by 1½ feet (0.6 by 0.4 m). Place a clean pebble
inside the bag to weigh down one corner. Now tie the bag
around the leafy branch of a tree or shrub in sunlight. Water
vapor transpires from the leaves, condenses on the inside of
the bag, and runs down toward the weighted corner. In one
experiment with a bag of the size mentioned and a branch of
a green ash tree, I recovered ⅓ cup (79 mL) of water. If you

① In this **solar tree still**, the plastic bag, 28 by 17 inches (711 by 432 mm), is tied
around a branch of green ash. ② One-third cup (79 mL) of water has collected in the
tree still's lower corner, which is weighted with a pebble.

carry several bags and set them all out, you can ensure a ready source of water with very little effort. From my experiments, solar tree stills don't harm the tree.

Solar Ground Still

If you had brought a 6-foot-square (1.8 m square) sheet of clear plastic (more likely in your vehicle than in your pack), and if you have the energy to dig a hole 3 feet across and 1½ feet deep (0.9 by 0.4 m), try extracting water from a solar ground still. Situate the hole, tapered toward the center, in moist or damp soil. To enhance your chances for water recovery, line the sides of the hole with green leaves, grass, or cacti stems. Place a wide-mouth container in the deepest part of the hole. Secure the plastic sheet over the rim of the hole with soil and rocks, and lay a fist-size or smaller pebble in the center of the sheet. This arrangement creates a cone-shaped plastic sheet, which should be aligned so the pebble is just above the container. The sheet should not touch the sides of the hole nor the container.

The sun's heat vaporizes the water in the soil and plants. The air saturates, and water vapor condenses on the underside of the plastic sheet, which is cooler than the damp air beneath it. Droplets run and fall into the container. The still also works

The hole for this **solar ground still** is 40 inches across and 20 inches deep (1.02 by 0.51 m), covered with a 6-foot-square (1.8 sq. m) sheet of clear plastic. A boy sips water from a container at the bottom of the still via plastic tubing.

at night because the soil remains warm and the plastic sheet is cooler.

Two modifications are useful. *If* you had also brought along a 5-foot (1.5 m) length of plastic tubing, you could have placed one end into the container and sip water as it collects without dismantling the still each time you desire a drink. Sometimes the droplets fall before reaching the container. Scratch the underside of the plastic with sand or sandstone in directions toward the pebble to guide the droplets directly to the container.

If all goes well, you might get a pint of water in a day. Recovery, of course, depends on the moistness of the soil and the amount of vegetation you may have placed in the hole. As water production drops off, move the still to a better site.

You may also use the still as a purifier. Dig a ring-shaped trough around the inside of the hole where you had first placed the vegetation. Take care to isolate the trough from the collecting container. Pour polluted water or urine into the trough. This approach allows you to gain watery benefit from unpalatable fluids.

Water from Snow and Ice

Don't eat snow or suck on ice if you have a choice; both cool the inner body too much. Melting them is the best option.

Choose snow from beneath the surface, which is more compact and yields more water than fluffy surface snow. If you have a cooking pot, pack in only a small amount of snow at a time. You don't want to burn the bottom of the pot. Once you gain a little water, leave some in the pot as you melt more snow. Another method is simply to place a hot rock in a container of snow. If fuel is plentiful, drink warm water or make tea.

Melting ice is a better choice because more water is recovered from a similar volume as compared with snow, and with less heat and less time. If you are in the Arctic and are dependent on sea ice, look for old sea ice, which is bluish and has rounded corners. Taste a small amount to ensure the ice contains little or no salt.

Should you lack a cooking pot, you can still recover meltwater from snow or ice. Place a hot rock in snow. Shove snow over the rock as it settles. Dip up or slurp up the water that collects above the rock. Try the same hot-rock approach on a frozen puddle or other ice surface. You might also try to heat snow or ice on a flat rock slab and have the water drain into a container.

If you have no fire nor cooking pot, you still have the means to recover meltwater, providing that you remembered to carry a black plastic sheet or bag. On a sunny day, lay the sheet or bag over a depression in the snow and scatter snow on the surface. The black color of the bag will absorb the heat of the sun and melt the snow.

PURIFYING WATER

Today, most natural surface waters are impure, as is much of the groundwater. Water is polluted largely by chemical or organic substances. You can't do much about chemical pollution except try to avoid water that may be contaminated by chemicals. Direct your main defense against the effects of such organic substances as feces and urine from sick humans or sick animals, which transmit disease through microscopic bacteria, viruses, and **protozoans** (single-celled animal-like organisms).

Waterborne diseases, among them giardiasis (*gee-are-DIE-uh-suhs*), amoebic dysentery, and typhoid fever, should not be taken lightly. Protozoan-caused giardiasis, known also as "backpackers' diarrhea" and one of the most common waterborne diseases in humans in the U.S., is notorious for causing victims to suffer extreme diarrhea. Other effects include abdominal cramps and nausea. The symptoms appear within one to two weeks and may last four to six weeks or longer. No fun. Also caused by a protozoan, amoebic dysentery leads to abdominal cramps and diarrhea, often bloody, which may last for a few weeks if not treated. Unpleasant symptoms of typhoid fever, caused by a bacterium, include vomiting, chills, fever, weakness, usually bloody diarrhea, and often delirium.

In order to avoid these and other waterborne diseases, you should be aware of basic purification methods. (If, however, the choice rests between drinking possibly impure water or immediate dehydration, you might choose the questionable water.) First, though, a few assumptions. Just because other mammals drink water from a particular source without ill effects doesn't mean you can. (The same goes for eating wild plants.) Springs, however, are usually pure, providing that you make a point of drinking from their actual sources. I also assume that you don't have a pump filter water purifier with you.

Before any attempt at purification, if the water is cloudy or muddy, filter it first through a cloth or allow the sediment to settle. Boiling, the traditional method and the one most used in emergencies, is reliable against bacteria, viruses, and proto-zoans if done with care. A common recommendation is to boil water for 5 minutes at sea level and 1 minute more for each 1,000 feet (305 m) of elevation. For added safety, I'd recommend boiling for at least 10 minutes at sea level, plus the additional minute for each 1,000 feet (305 m) of elevation.

For emergencies, I'd narrow down the chemical purification of water to one method, the use of tetraglycine hydroperiodide *(teh-truh-GLIE-seen high-droe-purr-EYE-uh-died)* in tablet form, available as the widely sold Potable Aqua and other similar products. Each tablet treats a pint of water. A 1-ounce bottle contains fifty tablets and can be easily carried with you. Be heedful that neither this method nor boiling protects you against chemical contaminants.

Don't forget, as already mentioned in this chapter, that a solar ground still can be used to purify polluted water. But, of course, in order to use this method you will need to bring the necessary materials.

PRACTICE FINDING WATER

As you might experiment with wild edible plants, you might practice finding water to become more knowledgeable and comfortable with your environment. Allow all the tips given in this chapter to work in concert. As you travel, predict where you expect water and check how many times you're right. Your success rate will improve as your guesses become more educated.

Try collecting water in several ways. Especially test the easy methods of collecting dew and rainwater and the use of a solar tree still. The best means are always those that require the least effort.

Evaluate the purity of any water source. You'll get better at this as you practice. Water tends to be safer at higher elevations and away from populated places, but don't assume that water is pure just because of its location. Be on the lookout for insidious effluents, and be aware that clear water often belies its purity.

Further Reading

Couplan, François. *Encyclopedia of Edible Plants of North America*. New Canaan CT: Keats Publishing, 1998. Gives uses of about 4,000 plants in Alaska, Canada, conterminous U.S., and northern Mexico. Not an identification manual, lacks plant descriptions. Line drawings of some plants.

Duke, James A. *Handbook of Edible Weeds*. Boca Raton: CRC Press, 2000. Covers one hundred plants or plant groups in the contiguous U.S. Illustrated by line drawings. Plants arranged alphabetically by scientific name.

Elias, Thomas S., and Peter A. Dykeman. *Edible Wild Plants: A North American Field Guide*. New York: Sterling, 1990. Covers more than two hundred plants, with maps of species in the U.S. and Canada. Mostly color photographs of plants.

Facciola, Stephen. *Cornucopia II. A Source Book of Edible Plants*. Vista CA: Kampong Publications, 1998. Part 1 lists about 3,000 plants, fungi, algae, and bacteria, arranged alphabetically by scientific names, and gives ways to eat them. Both wild and cultivated plants are included. Part 2 gives information on 110 major crops, arranged alphabetically by common names.

Gibbons, Euell. *Stalking the Wild Asparagus*. 25th anniversary ed. Putney VT: A.C. Hood, 1987. A classic that led to many other books by Gibbons. Good, appealing reading, crammed with many trustworthy recipes. Plants are arranged alphabetically by common names. Illustrated by line drawings. Also chapters on meat courses and one on herbal medicine.

Gibbons, Euell, and Gordon Tucker. *Euell Gibbons' Handbook of Edible Wild Plants*. Virginia Beach: Donning, 1979. Contains descriptions of about 260 plants or plant groups in the U.S. and Canada. Illustrated by shaded drawings.

Kershaw, Linda, Andy MacKinnon, and Jim Pojar. *Plants of the Rocky Mountains*. Edmonton AB: Lone Pine Publishing, 1998. Covers more than 1,300 hundred plants grouped as trees, shrubs, wildflowers, aquatics, grasslike plants, ferns and allies, mosses and liverworts, and lichens. Illustrated by numerous color photographs and line drawings. Many comments on edible and other uses of wild plants.

Kindscher, Kelly. *Edible Wild Plants of the Prairie: An Ethnobotanical Guide*. Lawrence: University Press of Kansas, 1987. Treats eighty-two plant species. Illustrated by line drawings with distribution maps; many species are not illustrated. Arranged alphabetically by scientific name.

Kirk, Donald R. *Wild Edible Plants of the Western United States, Including Also Most of Southwestern Canada and Northwestern Mexico*. Vol. 1. Healdsburg CA: Naturegraph Publishers, 1970. Treats about 2,000 edible plants, arranged by general geographic area, then by plant family. Illustrated by line drawings. Also a 1975 color edition with sixteen color plates.

McConnaughey, Evelyn. *Sea Vegetables: Harvesting Guide and Cookbook*. Happy Camp CA: Naturegraph Publishers, 1985. Covers many seaweeds on the Atlantic and Pacific Coasts of North America, arranged alphabetically by genus. Numerous recipes. Includes foraging tips. Illustrated by black-and-white photographs and line drawings.

Peterson, Lee Allen. *A Field Guide to Edible Wild Plants*. Boston: Houghton Mifflin, 1999. Reprint of 1978 edition. Covers nearly four hundred plant species, illustrated mostly by line drawings but with a selection of color photographs. Plants are variably arranged. Region covered is east of the 97th meridian.

Schofield, Janice J. *Alaska's Wild Plants: A Guide to Alaska's Edible Harvest*. Anchorage: Alaska Northwest Books, 1993. Covers more than seventy edible plants. Illustrated by color photographs. Also medicinal uses. Includes seven poisonous plants.

Tilford, Gregory L. *Edible and Medicinal Plants of the West*. Missoula MT: Mountain Press, 1997. Covers more than 250 plant species within the Northern Rockies to the coastal ranges of the Pacific Northwest and also Alaska and western Canada. Color photographs of plants.

Tull, Delena. *Edible and Useful Plants of Texas and the Southwest: Including Recipes, Harmful Plants, Natural Dyes, and Textile Fibers: A Practical Guide*. Austin: University of Texas Press, 1999. Many wild and naturalized plants of Texas used for food, dyes, fibers, medicine, and other uses. Also many poisonous plants. Most plants illustrated by line drawings, with a selection of color photographs.

Willard, Terry. *Edible and Medicinal Plants of the Rocky Mountains and Neighboring Territories*. Calgary AB: Wild Rose College of Natural Healing, 1992. 154 plant entries. Mostly color photographs with some line drawings. Small section on poisonous plants.

Young, Kay. *Wild Seasons: Gathering and Cooking Wild Plants of the Great Plains*. Lincoln: University of Nebraska Press, 1993. About fifty plants or plant groups covered, arranged by season when edible parts become available. Nearly 250 recipes. Illustrated by line drawings.

About the Author

ALAN M. CVANCARA HAS STUDIED AND PHOTOGRAPHED WILD edible plants since the late 1960s, spurred on by the appealing writings of that trustworthy forager Euell Gibbons. For nearly nine years, Cvancara experimented intensively with wild edible plants on a Minnesota farm retreat and has presented numerous talks on the subject, illustrated with his photographs. He continues his work with edible plants while living in Wyoming, transplanted from his native North Dakota.

Although trained as a geologist—he is Professor Emeritus of Geology from the University of North Dakota—he considers himself a naturalist. He is the published author of four other nature books: *A Field Manual for the Amateur Geologist: Tools and Activities for Exploring Our Planet*; *Sleuthing Fossils: The Art of Investigating Past Life*; *At the Water's Edge: Nature Study in Lakes, Streams, and Ponds*; and *Exploring Nature in Winter: A Guide to Activities, Adventures, and Projects for the Winter Naturalist*.

ML   12/02